GOD,
A WOMAN,
AND
THE WAY

MEDIATOR
AND
MEDIATRIX

REV. FR. RAYMOND, O.C.S.O.

ILLUSTRATED BY JOHN ANDREWS

 Distributed by:
ANGELUS PRESS
2918 Tracy Ave
Kansas City, MO 64109 USA
1-800-966-7337 • 1-816-753-3150

SARTO HOUSE

NIHIL OBSTAT:
   Fr. M. Paul Bourne, O.C.S.O.
   Fr. M. Augustine Westland, O.C.S.O.
   Censores

IMPRIMI POTEST:
   Most Rev. Dom M. Gabriel Sortais, O.C.S.O.
   Abbas Generalis

NIHIL OBSTAT:
   John A. Schelien, S.T.D.
   Censor librorum

IMPRIMATUR:
   +Albert G. Meyer
   Archiepiscopus Milwauchiensis

Die 13a Decembris, 1954

Unless otherwise noted the Scripture text used in this book is that of the Confraternity edition for the New Testament and of the Douay for the Old Testament.

Originally published by The Bruce Publishing Company.

Catholic University of America Classification:
Lynn, BQT2598.D6   Dewey, 232.931
Library of Congress Catalog Card Number: 55-7112

Reprinted and retypeset by Sarto House from the Second Printing (1956).

SARTO HOUSE
PO Box 270611
Kansas City, MO 64127-0611

ISBN   0-9639032-5-X
First Printing—January 2000

Printed in the United States of America.

TO
OUR IMMACULATE MOTHER
MARY
AND
HER OBLATE SON
MY BROTHER
FR. EDDIE, O.M.I.

Other Works by
REV. M. RAYMOND, O.C.S.O.

The Less Traveled Road

The Man Who Got Even With God

God Goes to Murderers' Row

A New Way of the Cross

Trappists, The Reds, and You

Three Religious Rebels

The Family That Overtook Christ

Burnt Out Incense

Some Women of Citeaux

Booklets

Is Your Home Like This?

Running off With God

Life Is Someone

Are You

FIAT! Remake Your World

Life Is a Divine Romance

Set the World on Fire

For Your Own Defense

What Are You Doing to Jesus Christ

A Message From Those Killed in
    Action

Doubling for the Mother of God

Whispers from the Wings (Sequel)

Do You Want Life and Love?

A Startling Thing for You

Have You Met God?

Facts About Reason, Revelation and
    Religion

To Mothers Whose Sons Are in the
    Service

The God-Man's Double

What's Wrong?

Help God Be a Success

You Are Leading a Dangerous Life

Acknowledgments

Acknowledgment is gratefully made to the following publishers, authors, and others controlling copyrights who have permitted the use of quotations: to The Bruce Publishing Company for passages from *The New Testament* in the translation of James A. Kleist, S.J., and Joseph L. Lilly, C.M.; to Msgr. Hugh F. Blunt for "The Guilty One"; to E. P. Dutton and Company for the lines from "The Wild Knight," by G. K. Chesterton; to James M. Gillis, C.S.P., and Charles Scribner's Sons for a passage from *So Near Is God: Essays on the Spiritual Life;* to the Macmillan Company for lines from *A Woman Wrapped in Silence,* by John W. Lynch; to Sheed and Ward for passages from the *Old Testament,* Vol. II, and the *New Testament* in the translation of Msgr. Ronald Knox, for a passage from *The Water and the Fire,* by Gerald Vann, O.P., and for passages from *The Mary Book,* edited by Frank Sheed; and to Charles L. Wallis and Harper and Brothers for "Between Midnight and Morning," by Owen Seaman, in *Masterpieces of Religious Verse.*

Contents

About the Author

The work of Rev. Fr. M. Raymond, O.C.S.O. (a.k.a. Rev. Fr. Joseph David Flanagan) was principally about contemplatives and their struggle for sainthood. His remarkable success was due to the fact that, apart from his learning and literary skill, he held tenaciously to the opinion that saints are to be emulated, not just admired. Saints, he believed, should be shown to be humans with difficulties such as are experienced by all of us.

Fr. Raymond's career, first at college and then as a Jesuit, led up to when he became a Cistercian of the Strict Observance (1936). It was then, as he explained, in silence and in solitude, that he was able to live what he learned as a son of St. Ignatius. "Perhaps," he added, "I'll become a cloistered contemplative in earnest only when cloistered in heaven and contemplating the Beauty 'ever ancient, ever new.'"

Born in Roxbury, Massachusetts, in 1903, he was baptized Joseph David, to which names he subsequently added "Stanislaus" through admiration of the Polish Jesuit boy-saint. His first teachers were the daughters of Mother Seton. He graduated from Boston College High School with sports honors. He entered the novitiate of the Society of Jesus in 1920 and there was trained by two distinguished literature priest-professors who developed his imagination and fine sense of rhetoric and expression.

From 1927-30, the future Fr. Raymond held the Chair

of Rhetoric at Holy Cross College, Worcester, Massachusetts. During these years he was Moderator of the Holy Cross Debating Societies and developed teams that achieved fame. His period as a missioner and retreat master were at the end of his career in the Society of Jesus. In 1936, he entered the cloister of the Abbey of Our Lady of Gethsemane in Kentucky, the first abbey established in the United States.

Among the published works of Fr. Raymond are the following: *The Man Who Got Even with God; The Life of an American Trappist* (Brother Joachim, 1941); *The Saga of Citeaux* (First Epoch); *Three Religious Rebels, Forefathers of the Trappists* (1944); *The Saga of Citeaux* (Second Epoch); *The Family That Overtook Christ* (1942); *The Saga of Citeaux* (American Epoch); *Burnt Out Incense* (1949); and *God Goes to Murderer's Row* (1951). In addition he wrote 20 booklets.

Fr. Raymond's central idea was the doctrine of the Mystical Body of Christ. In everything he wrote this doctrine was illustrated. He claimed that it was not only the heart of theology, but the only satisfying explanation of life, since it gives man his true dignity, his destiny, and points out his duty.

In *Burnt Out Incense*, man's true dignity and destiny, when he takes up the contemplative life, are justified. This story of the first hundred years of Trappist life in Kentucky moves the mind and heart profoundly. This book epitomizes well what the Cistercians of the Strict Observance do—giving their lives, burning themselves out that souls may be holy as God wants them to be holy. The reader is carried away by the story of heroic sanctity, of trials, of privations, and hardships that are as much the foundations of the Abbey of Our Lady of Gethsemane as the bricks and mortar that went into its building.

Our Hope

IN THE HANDS OF A WOMAN

HOLY WEEK for a Trappist is something tremendous. It is the noisiest of all the weeks in his swift, silent cycle of fifty-two. For he opens it with "*Hosannas*" that once shook the City of Jerusalem, and closes it with "*Alleluias*" that have shaken the centuries, and will ever shake the City of God. But what lies between shakes the Trappist's very soul.

We monks are contemplatives. Now that means only one thing. It means that we are under serious and holy obligation to strive ever *to live in Christ Jesus*. In recent years much has been written on contemplation; but I fear there has been altogether too much brilliance and too little light, so we look for clarity in vain. Yet, Augustine summed the whole thing up in three words long centuries ago. He simply said: *Vivere in Verbo*. There you have the essence and even the quintessence of the contemplative life. There you have the complete description of a contemplative. He is one who strives ever to *live in the Word*. Imagine, if you can, what that means to us monks in Holy Week, when you realize that Jesus is the Word.

Jesus was a contemplative. From Him undoubtedly, and perhaps in Holy Week, Augustine got his definition and description. For it is in this week that Christ takes the center of the stage and shows us, as never before, just what a contemplative is and what a contemplative does. You and I and all our fellow men were the object of Christ's contemplation. Looking on us, He loved us. Loving us, nothing short of absolute union would satisfy Him. Such is ever the way with those who love truly. So He took upon Himself all that was in us—even the shape and color of our sins. That shape became the shape of a cross; that color, the rich crimson of His blood that stained it.

With that example before us, there is only one thing we Trappists can do in Holy Week. We must live over every hour of every day with the Christ. We must live every instant in Him—thus coming to know His passionateness even before we know His Passion. This is the week we see Christ's character crystallized in His actions. Sunday the very stones are ready to cry out: "Hosanna to the Son of David," as a meek and gentle Jesus rides over them amid waving palm branches while garments are strewn on His way. But before high noon, that same Jesus, in holy fury, is scourging the money-changers from the Temple, and before dusk is weeping over a City that "would not" and pronouncing a doom that surely would be. Monday early He comes over from Bethany. He sees a fig tree by the road. He goes up to it; finds it all foliage and no fruit; He curses it, and the thing withers. He enters the Temple. Round Him gather the chief priests and the elders of the people. With subtle questions they try to catch Him. His answer is the blood-freezing prediction that "Publicans and harlots are entering the Kingdom of Heaven before you..." Think of it: publicans and harlots before the chief priests and elders of His chosen people! That night, back at Bethany, there is a banquet. At it an alabaster box is broken. A thief and a traitor asks the question so often asked about us Trappists: "Why this woeful waste?"—and a loving girl is made immortal as an all-loving God says: "Let her be. She hath anointed My Body for the burial."—Yesterday the people were ready to make Him king; today He and a girl ready His body for burial.

Tuesday He is back in the Temple. His oldest and fiercest
foes crowd in on Him. With eight "Woes"—the mere
reading of which makes brave men blanche even today—
He blasts them. "Woe to you Scribes and Pharisees.
Hypocrites!" That night on His way back to Bethany, He
stops at the brow of the hill and again foretells the doom
which is to fall on the City. Wednesday He is alone with
His Father—Judas is alone with the high priests. Thursday
—O, Great God, such wonders!—the Eucharist—the
Priesthood—the Mass! Then comes Friday...Friday...And
yet we call it "Good."

The liturgy as lived at Gethsemani during Holy Week
brings us closer to God than ever Moses came by the burning bush or even in the covering cloud. For it telescopes
Time, takes us out of the twentieth century and places us
prostrate in the Garden by the side of the young priest
who is contemplating his first Mass and shrinking back
from the soul-shaking ordeal. It drags us prisoners to the
hall of Caiphas, has soldiers spit in our faces and mock us
as the Sanhedrin waits the dawn so that we can be hauled
before Pilate. We are robed as fools and set at naught by
Herod and his court. We are scourged....By Friday afternoon most of us monks stagger about our cloisters like
drunken men; for, in us, our hearts beat like some slow,
solemn bell, sending along our trembling veins the one
refrain: "Jesus, our Love, is crucified!"

Truly this is "The Great Week"...In it the liturgy shows
us love and life. Too often people think the liturgy but
recalls the past. Instead, the liturgy treats of the present
moment ever! With exquisite preciseness it tells that it was
at the ninth hour, on the fourteenth day of the month
Nisan, that Jesus died on Calvary about the year AD 33.
Yet, even with greater preciseness does it say that that hour
is eternal, unending, ever present. Actually, it is ever recalling to mind these words of Leon Bloy: "Jesus is always
being crucified, always bleeding, always expiring, always

mocked by the populace and cursed by God Himself in accord with the precise wording of the Ancient Law: 'He that hangeth on the tree is cursed of God.'" With each dawn it makes us realize with Pascal that "Jesus Christ will be in Agony until the end of the world." And thus we, who live the liturgy, can never forget that we are His members with a work to do. We must remind ourselves of Paul's words: "...what is lacking of the sufferings of Christ I fill up in my flesh for his body, which is the Church" (Col. 1:24).

GOD'S TACTICS And God keeps us conscious of the fact that the liturgy treats of the here and now. For cloistered though we are from the world, He never allows us to forget that He "so loved the world that he gave his only begotten son," for it (Jn. 3:16). So jealous is He of the honor He would have from us monks that He is continually reminding us of the special work we have to do *in Christ Jesus*. It is not enough to have His Son's vicars write stirring encyclicals telling the power that lies in our prayer and the responsibility to complete His Passion that rests on our hearts, but God is so determined that we shall never forget, that He extends His ordinary Providence and bas-reliefs the role Trappists must play in the great drama of the Redeeming by sending us, every now and then, from most unexpected sources, but always at the opportune moment, witnesses who testify to the fact that His body bleeds...and His Mother weeps.

From behind both communist curtains have come to us unmartyred martyrs to tell not only what they had suffered for Christ but more especially what we monks must undergo for Christians. Since we look upon every event in our lives as a "coming of Christ," you can readily understand why we listened to these men as we would to the God-Man. They had a message for us from the heart of God. They said: *"Christ needs you."*

Just before Holy Week of 1954, God sent us an aged bishop and his middle-aged vicar-general, men who had been released but recently from two torturous years of captivity under the Chinese Reds. Last year, at Passiontide, He sent us a young priest who had undergone "the Passion"—all but the crucifixion. The arrest, the imprisonment, the mock trials, the blows, scourging, spittle, and something like the thorns were all there. Not long after that we listened to one who had had his "brain washed" by the Communists. How sharply do such events say: "Gethsemani's agony was not only on the night of the 14th day of the month Nisan about the year AD 33. It goes on...."

Thus does God speak to us. Thus do we come to know that in China Christ has been before Pilate and Herod, has stumbled to the Hill of Skulls, and is now naked and nailed to His cross; while in Russia the fifth of His Seven Last Words has already lighted the dark: *Eli, Eli, lema sabacthani?* (Mt. 27:46.) Perhaps, by now, He is already dead.

Yet each of these unmartyred martyrs, both prelate and priests, spoke much more of a Resurrection than they did of death and burial. Each was enthusiastic and highly optimistic about the future. Though they had come from a land that is black with hate and evil, where no candle may be lit for the Mass, these men saw nothing but bright promise for the morrow; for each, somehow or other, had seen all that John Andrews has shown us in these drawings. They said exactly what I am going to say: *Our hope lies in the hands of a woman!*

I spent Holy Week with her.

All my life I have wondered where Mary was these early hours of the Passion. Was she at the Last Supper? Did she receive her First Holy Communion from the hands of Him to whom she had given the white wheat of her own flesh that He might have a body and the rich, red wine from her inmost vein that He might have blood? Was she present at the first ordination of priests in the New Law?

Where was she while He was sweating in the Garden? While He was sport for the spittle of the guards after Peter had denied Him and the high priests condemned Him, was it Magdalen who drew a blanket over our Lady's shoulders as she stirred perhaps in uneasy rest? And on the morrow...where was she when Pilate washed his hands and the Jews cried for His blood upon themselves and their children?

Some silences of Scripture can stir a man to his soul's center. These have always stirred me. But this year the drawings of an American artist filled all the silences left by the Holy Ghost and revealed to me that the *Via Matris* is parallel to the road it meets—the *Via Dolorosa;* that two truths are really one: *We are His members* and *She is our Mother;* that there is a way out of the modern cul-de-sac; that there is light in our age of blackout, and bright, brilliant hope for a world growing ever more hopeless.

It is she.

Spes Nostra—Our Hope. That is what she has been called for centuries; and that is what more than four hundred million Catholics call her today. *Spes Nostra* is the title Trappists give her each day as shadows deepen and stars begin to silver the dark. "Our Hope" is what God Himself would have the whole world name her in this hour which seems so utterly devoid of hope. For if that "dance of the sun," seen by 70,000 at Fatima on October 13, 1917—a sight which sent them to their knees, beating their breasts, and crying aloud for mercy—means anything, it means that in this dark and ever darkening hour we can have hope in this "Lady of Light."

Hydrogen need not destroy us. This "Woman clothed with the sun" can save! Hate need not completely corrode our civilization nor lust for power wreck our Western world. This "Mother of Fair Love" can heal hearts; this "Seat of Wisdom," bring sanity to the most insane of men.

Many are the titles given to Mary. Each has been

earned—paid for with a great price as she walked this Way. But for us of the mid-twentieth century none, perhaps, is as timely or telling as *Salus Infirmorum*—"Health of the Sick." For modern man is ill, very, very ill. Yet, of the countless attending physicians, who has so much as named the disease aright? It is not economic, as so many of them have said. Neither is it purely social or simply political as others would have us believe. Modern man is sick with a disease that lies deeper than any of these symptoms indicate.

To the monk hidden behind high cloisters it is well known that man as man is more than an economic unit, a political pawn, or a social being. He knows that man, in his innermost essence, is a hunger for happiness, a desert-thirst for truth, a restless, relentless, insatiable gnawing for the beautiful. So in the face of the learned diagnoses of the professionals, the simple monk dares to say that modern man is suffering from a malignancy that may well cause his death; and he names it a *nostalgia for God* which has been brought on by an *amnesia* of the dignity of man.

Far from denying the existence of economic evils, social ills, and political sicknesses, that diagnosis admits each of them. Modern man is sick all over. But what appears on the surface has source in his soul. Never has psychosomatics been more clearly demonstrated. The disorders that strike the eye are strictly psychogenic. What has spilled over into the body politic and is made so manifest in the social and economic organism wells up from the deeply disordered mind and heart of modern man. It is a disorder that makes our world truly psychotic. But though the illness be mental, the real source of the trouble is not in the mind. Freud, Adler, Jung, and Meyer notwithstanding, the focus of infection lies neither in the subconscious nor in the unconscious, It is found fully on the surface of man's self-consciousness. The "primary" of the world-wide sickness of the day, a pathology that could well prove fatal, is seated in man's *memory*. That is why I have called it *amnesia* and why I say it demands treatment far different from what has been given.

Most of the attending physicians have been busy treating symptoms, without ever once touching the source of the disease. They have lanced boils when they should have purged the blood. They have put cold packs to a feverish brow, when they should have been seeking the cause of the fever and routing it out of the body. Sedatives can never take the place of surgery, nor temporary relief satisfy one who wants a permanent cure. Why filter dirty water when we can clean the well?

While studying these drawings by John Andrews of the hands of a woman who lived and died 2,000 years ago, I suddenly found myself staring into the eyes of modern man.

I found many lights there; few of them fully healthy. The cold gleam of fear is there; the low, dull glints of frustration and defeat; the steely sparks of worry and frightening flashes of anxiety. But deeper than any, and glowing over all, is the mad light of desperation.

Modern psychiatrists would set about probing the subconscious and even the unconscious, searching for the flints that have struck up these flames. But the source of all these fires is *forgetfulness*. Modern man has forgotten his origin and his end; forgotten his dignity and destiny; forgotten his innate nobility and towering superiority over everything material. Modern man with his vaunted progress reminds one forcibly of that traveler Marcus Aurelius told about; the one who was feverishly hurrying on, but had forgotten where he was going. Modern man has outdone this one; for modern man has forgotten even whence he set out. He has forgotten that he is a man and not a machine, the masterpiece of visible creation and not the product of blind forces, an immortal living in time, an

exile with a home in a far country, a breath of God in a
vessel of clay. He has forgotten his own identity and his
essence. That is the amnesia which must be cured. It is
man's memory, not man's mind, that demands the treatment. If he can be made to bring to the surface of his consciousness the true concept of what he is, modern madness
ends. The patient cures himself. And the cure lies in correct self-consciousness.

Here precisely is where the drawings of John Andrews **THE CURE**
come in; for we will never know what we are, nor come to
an estimate of our real worth, until we have studied what
the hands of this woman hold and walked the Way she and
He walked. Contemplation issues in action. If we sit silent
before these hands, memory will stir, and soon our minds
will be dwelling on the only great facts of history. Then the
trifles that so disturb the present times will be seen in
proper perspective and the wild lights that have blazed in
our eyes will fade as our whole face becomes flushed with
the joy and expectation that illumines the countenance of
a child when he looks on his loving and greatly loved
mother.

Children learn fear. That is what all psychologists say.
Why, then, cannot we adults unlearn it?

By that I do not mean to intimate that every man
should be without a single semblance of fear; for it is only
the fool who is completely without dread, just as it is only
the fool that "hath said in his heart: There is no God" (Ps.
13:1). But from that anxious fear which has the modern
world cringing, from that all-pervading dread which can
paralyze a man mentally as well as physically, from that
all-too-prevalent attitude of mind which, if it becomes
habitual, leads inevitably either to a recklessness which
plunges us into ruin or to an apathy which invites the
same to overtake us—from all that, I say, we can be freed.
All we need do is stir our memories and let them stimulate
our minds! For at the root of all this needless worry, this

unnerving sense of insecurity, this fear which ultimately will unman a man, lies forgetfulness. We forget too much history—and very particularly the sacred history that we commemorate in Holy Week. We forget what happened to Jesus, the Light of the World, "from the sixth hour...until the ninth hour"; we forget that "there was darkness over the whole land"; we forget that "about the ninth hour Jesus...cried out with a loud voice, and gave up his spirit" (Mt. 27:45-51).

If we would only remember that little bit, we would come to see it is not man's ability to split the atom which should cause us fear, but only his ability to split the heart of Him who made the atom. If this fear once takes possession of us, we will find that we are free of all other fears.

I say that, cognizant of America's and Russia's possession of the H-bomb. I say that fully aware of the fact that scientists have said that man now possesses "the power to destroy the universe." There I pause and smile; for I remember the first lines of Genesis: "In the beginning God created heaven and earth..." and I cannot help thinking that since it was God who created the universe, and since it has been God who has kept it in being all these years and aeons, it will be God, and only God, who will bring it to an end. I do not think any man is going to surprise God—not even the communist, who claims there is no God!

And now a whole flood of memories causes my smile to broaden....Do you remember the proud and presumptuous men at Babel who had learned to bake bricks when "the earth was of one tongue, and of the same speech"? (Gen. 11:1) They would build a tower that would reach to heaven. Do you remember how God watched them for some time building their city and their tower? Then He came down—and we got a word for confusion!

Do you recall the Second Psalm? We monks sing it the second day of every week. We open Monday morning with a Sunrise Song, which begins: "*Quare fremuerunt gentes*—Why are the Nations of the world so foolishly in tumult?"—"*et populi meditati sunt inania*—and why are the peoples of the earth devising such empty, vain, and stupid things?" Though David wrote those words thirty centuries ago, they are apt enough for headlines in our mid-twentieth century's daily papers.

Could not the New York *Times,* the Boston *Post,* the Chicago *Tribune,* the St. Louis *Post-Dispatch,* the San Francisco *Chronicle,* or any of our leading papers have used David's second verse as headlines almost any day since the dawn of this mad century? "*Astiterunt reges terrae, et principes convenerunt in unum adversus Dominum et adversus Christum ejus*—The kings of the earth stand in array, and its rulers make common cause against the Lord and against his Christ," crying "*dirumpamus vincula eorum*—Let us break their bonds asunder and cast from us their yoke." True, ten hundred years before Christ, it appears even more true twenty hundred years after Him. But—and here is where the smiles come in—the Psalm goes on to say: "*Qui habitat in coelis irridebit eos*—He that dwelleth in heaven shall laugh at them."

We have made A-bombs and H-bombs. We are very proud and quite presumptuous. We, dwellers in modern Babylon! But the same God who was amused at the little men who made bricks is laughing at the men who now make bombs. And in His own good time He will come down and show us how right Browning was.

A white fist on a red flag shakes itself angrily at the face of the One it says does not exist, and I hear David singing: "*Qui habitat in coelis irridebit eos....*" I hear Browning singing: "God's in His Heaven—all's right with the world." Memory can cure much insanity. They give electric shock treatment to make some patients forget. It seems to me that God is giving us electric shock treatment to make us remember.

I had occasion to read some of the Prophets recently and I could not but think that, save for the swing of the language, I was reading *Time* or *Life* or *Newsweek*. The things that are newsworthy today are anything but new. Dictators are older, far older, than the fall of Rome—or even its founding. Concentration camps were common when Moses was in the bullrushes. Slave labor built the pyramids, put the smile on the Sphinx, and made Babylon's Hanging Gardens a genuine wonder of the world. And when moderns were decrying the furnaces at Dachau I wanted to remind them to read the Book of Daniel.

Much of the senseless fear, which has us looking over our shoulder so often, would vanish if we would but remember the dream Nabuchodonosor had. The colossuses of earth may have heads of gold, arms of silver, thighs of brass, but their feet are always clay. And if we have to face fiery furnaces we can recall the song of Sidrach, Misach, and Abdenago. We Trappists sing it at least twice daily, and every priest is supposed to say it privately as he comes in from offering his Mass. The midst of any furnace can be made "like the blowing of a wind bringing dew," and the fire need not "touch, trouble, or harm" us; for God is still God and the mightiest of men His poor, weak creature.

We forget that song that burst from the throats of the three youths in that furnace: "*Benedicite omnia opera Domini Domino*—Bless ye the Lord *all* ye works of God"—atom and hydrogen, jet plane and guided missile....Bless ye the Lord!

THE LATEST NEWS   Despite the unquestionable prowess of the Associated Press and the United Press, despite the uncanny insights of many a news commentator, despite our lucid newscasts over radio and television, we still do not know what is going on. The facts and figures are given us. We not only hear, we see. We are seated not only on the sidelines and

at the ringside, but are taken into the ring and onto the
field by the telescopic lens. We are not brought to the
scene of the happening, the scene, even as it is happening,
is brought to our homes—and still we do not know what
is going on. For *we forget!* We forget that "not a hair of our
head falls without God's permission; that in His hands
dictators, presidents, prime ministers and kings are as
pawns; and that behind the curtain of appearances week
by week, day by day, minute by minute GOD controls the
whole scenario of the centuries and the years...."

Here is the latest news of the day—news for tomorrow
and the next day. It is taken from the mouth of a man who
had his lips burnt clean by God. It tells exactly what is
going on *now.* "Forasmuch [saith the Lord] as this people
hath cast away the waters of Siloe, that go with silence,
and hath rather taken Rasin, and the son of Romelia:
Therefore behold the Lord will bring upon them the waters
of the river strong and many, the king of the Assyrians,
and all his glory: and he shall come up over all his chan-
nels, and shall overflow all his banks, and shall pass
through Juda, overflowing, and going over shall reach even
to the neck. And the stretching out of his wings shall fill
the breadth of thy land, O Emmanuel" (Is. 8:6-8.
Emphasis added). Supply "Dictator of the Russians" for
"King of the Assyrians," change the figure of "flood" to
that of "curtains"—with which we are so familiar—and
you have the latest news that needs no commentator.

Go on to the twelfth and thirteenth verses of the same
chapter and read: "Not for thee and thine to go in fear,
dismayed like these others; enthrone the Lord of Hosts
above all else, Him you must fear, of Him stand in awe.
Let the hour of peril consecrate you to him."[1] There is the
prescription for the present moment, the whole purpose of
the peril that is so real, but of which we need have no fear:
the patient cures himself.

Let us admit our amnesia and set about its cure by

---

[1] Knox translation. Emphasis added.

remembering—remembering Pharaoh, Assyria, Nabucho-donosor, the Medes and the Persians, Greece and Rome; remembering the lessons of Genesis and Job, the Patriarchs and the Prophets; always remembering the Commandments given to Moses and the promises given by Christ!

THE "FORMULA FOR SURVIVAL"

We have summed up the sickness in a word: *amnesia.* We can sum up the prescription in another word: *metanoia.* It "does seem as if "the Greeks had a word for it" always, does it not? Yet that prescription was given lately by none other than the father of relativity, the man whose equation finally gave us the A-bomb. Professor Albert Einstein has said that the real problem facing moderns is not atomic power nor its mechanism, but rather the ability of men—and very specifically of American men—to *change their minds and hearts!* That has been called the "formula for survival." And no one can question its ability to save if it is faithfully followed; for it is the formula given by God Himself as we read in Scripture from Genesis to the Apocalypse, but nowhere more forcefully than in the New Testament where *metanoia* rings like a refrain. John the Baptist used it. Jesus Himself used it again and again. And Peter's first sermon, which was climaxed by a mass conversion, was nothing but a call to a complete change of mind and heart.

We have taken that word bodily into our English language, but too few of us remember that, not only in Greek, but also in English, its basic meaning is "to change one's mind with regard to one's conduct."

How will we apply this "formula for survival"? How will we bring about this complete change of our minds and hearts?—By remembering! By remembering all that these pictures of John Andrews suggest.

You have noticed of course that when a child is afraid it will run to its mother, but when the child is in danger, it is the mother who runs—and she runs to her child. That is the whole meaning of the many apparitions of Mary with which the past century, or century and a half, has been blessed. We "children of a larger growth" were too sophisticated to be wise; we were not afraid of the very real dangers that threatened us. So our Lady-Mother ran to us in 1830 by appearing to Catherine Laboure in Paris. Sixteen years later she was found weeping at LaSalette, begging her children to "change their minds and hearts." That is the meaning of her "Pray and do penance!" For no one prays unless he remembers he is but a man. No one does penance unless be remembers that God is outraged by sin. So *Mary came to cure our amnesia.* In 1858 she was in the Grotto of Massabielle, near Lourdes, praying the Rosary with Bernadette and using the one word "Penitence." Twelve years later she blazoned the sky over Pontmain with the burning plea: *Donc, priez mes enfants!* And in our own century, in our own lifetime, did she not come on the 13th of every month from May to October to that lonely place in Portugal, appearing as the Lady of Light, who asked but one thing of men—a *metanoia—prayer* and penance?

There is something exquisitely tender in this sending of God's Mother to us of this mad twentieth century. She is sent at a time when our sins have merited a flood or Sodom's fire; when our heedlessness of God cries for a Jeremias or an Ezechiel; when our criminal forgetfulness of our Creator and our creatureship calls for a Nathan, an Amos or an Osee, or anyone of those other prophets who foretold the justice and judgments of God. She comes at a time when the world is pagan and does not know it! When it is worshiping Mars, Mammon, and Moloch—and does not know it! When Venus, Bacchus, and Priapus have been placed far forward in the modern Pantheon—and moderns know not that they have such gods or such a gallery; when all America has as its idol what Lloyd Morris rightly called the "bitch-goddess"—Success. She comes to us from heaven as "Our Life, Our Sweetness, and Our Hope!" She is not a Prophet, but the Queen of the Prophets. She comes not with threats of vengeance, but promises of peace, not foretelling our destruction, but our restoration if we will but have a *metanoia;* if we will but *remember....*

The rich man—who could well be taken as a figure of modern America—cried to God to send to earth someone to warn his brothers. And God said: "They have Moses and the Prophets, let them hearken to them" (Lk. 16:29). How well He could have said the same to us and of us. But, no. He sends us His mother and ours. Let us mistake not the purpose.

When one reads the prophets closely he notices that, despite their many differences, they have one thing in common; each is sent to write, as it were, on the memories of God's people what God Himself wrote on the marble Moses brought to the top of the mountain. What did Isaias, Jeremias, Ezechiel, Daniel, and the rest have to say but: *I am the Lord thy God: Thou shalt not have strange gods before me....*

It is the First Commandment that men forget—and upon which God ever insists. He has to, if He be God.

Let us remember that those who were brought out of Egypt and through the Red Sea were denied entrance into the Promised Land—because they forgot their God. Let us remember that the scourge of Assyria came upon Israel—because they forgot God. Let us remember that the Jews of the Kingdom of Juda were carried off to Babylon—because they forgot God. Let us remember that the very Temple which God filled with His glory was desecrated—because priests and people forgot God! The Chosen People had a Holy City, crowned with a Temple in which was the Holy of Holies, yet the veil in that Temple was rent and the Holy of Holies exposed; the Romans came and there was not left a stone upon stone of that Holy City; and the

Chosen People were scattered among the nations—because the First Commandment was not kept first.

We Gentiles have become the Chosen People of God. But now we dwell in Babylon! Yes, and the thinkers of our day have raised for themselves with their erring thoughts what Dietrich von Hildebrand has called "A New Tower of Babel"—it is all confusion! And why are we beset by Communism? Is it not because we have failed to remember that *He* said: "I am the Lord thy God. Thou shalt not have strange gods before me"?

We are in Babylon—but in His mercy He sends us His Mother.

We are in Babylon, but there is no reason why we cannot be like the Ninevites. You know the story of the capital of Assyria. God commanded His prophet, Jonas: "Up and to the great city of Nineve...great guilt of theirs claims my cognizance." Jonas did not want to go. He took ship for Tharsis "to be out of the Lord's way." But that was not to be. "The Lord sent out a boisterous wind, that raised a great tempest, and the ship was likely to be broken all in pieces" (Jonas 1:2,3).[2] Jonas went to Nineve; but not by ship. In the midst of that city he cried: "In forty days Nineve will be overthrown."

Now never forget that Nineve was a pagan land.

"And a cry was raised in Nineve, at the bidding of the King and the nobles, A fast for men and beasts...no food is to be eaten, no water drunk...cry out lustily to the Lord, and forsake, each of you, his sinful life, his wrongful deeds! God may yet relent and pardon....

"When God saw them amending their lives in good earnest, he spared them" (Jonas 3:5-10).[3]

Their metanoia won mercy!

The rest of the story is not only highly amusing; it is highly encouraging. Jonas got angry. He "told God off." But in doing so gave us every reason for hope; gave us every reason to become Ninevites in our modern Babylon.

---

[2] Knox translation.

[3] Knox translation.

"See," cried Jonas, "I knew it...I knew from the first what manner of God thou art, how kind and merciful, how slow to punish, how quick to pardon, vengeance ever ready to forego" (Jonas 4:2).[4]

Jonas wanted to die, so put out was he with God and His merciful ways. But if we want to live we will remember Jonas; we will remember that Christ pointed to him when the Jews wanted a sign; we will remember that Incarnate Truth said: "The men of Nineve will rise up in the judgment with this generation, and will condemn it; for they repented [had a *metanoia*] at the preaching of Jonas. And behold, a greater than Jonas is here" (Mt. 12:41).

One far greater than Jonas is here. The Queen of all Prophets. The very Mother of God. What tenderness on the part of Omnipotence!

THE QUEEN OF THE WORLD'S LAST CHANCE Yet in that very tenderness there is a terrifying element. Mary is the Queen of the Prophets and the Mother of God. The fact that it is she who comes to us makes it look as if the plea of Dives, the rich man, won hearing from God; makes it look as if no angel, archangel, prophet, or saint would do.

We can co-operate with Providence and heighten our hopes if we but remember some very forceful facts. When tempted to shudder at the name Malenkov and mention of the Reds, remember the Mongul, Genghis Kahn, and his powerful Tartars. In the early thirteenth century, without jet planes or atomic artillery, he and they swept from northern China clear across Europe to where your Iron Curtain halts today. He did it in half the time it has taken Russia. But Genghis Kahn and his Tartars passed away. When news of the stock piles of bombs that the Communists have erected reaches you, remember, Suleiman the Magnificent and his tremendous Turks. Early in the sixteenth century they repeated the history of the Tartars and Kahn. But in 1571, before Don Juan of

---

[4] Knox translation.

Austria and his much smaller force down went a seemingly unconquerable fleet. When stories of the potency latent
in cobalt come to frighten you, remember Sobieski and
Vienna in 1683. God is still God, and Mary is His
Mother. The Rosary can effect today what it did in the sixteenth and seventeenth centuries. Prayer can prove as powerful now as it did when the Tartars on their shaggy little
steeds threatened to destroy Western civilization. Mary
wants us to win, and she shows us *the way.*

John Andrews makes her Way unforgettable in the
hands and feet he has so reverently drawn. I ask the reader to look, long, and with an active mind. If the spiritual
message does not come from the white hands of the purest
woman who ever lived on our dusty, dirty earth, look
longer at the feet of Him who left bloodstained footprints
on this Way.

The dogma of the infinite value of each individual
human being is before us. God and God's Mother have
walked parallel Ways for the eternal happiness of every one
of us. Those parallel Ways met. That is why each of us can
be utterly fearless though skies fall, continents disappear,
oceans dry up; for we can walk the Way that leads to everlasting peace!

Look until your forgetfulness of the only things worth
remembering is utterly cured.

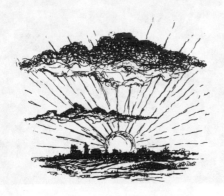

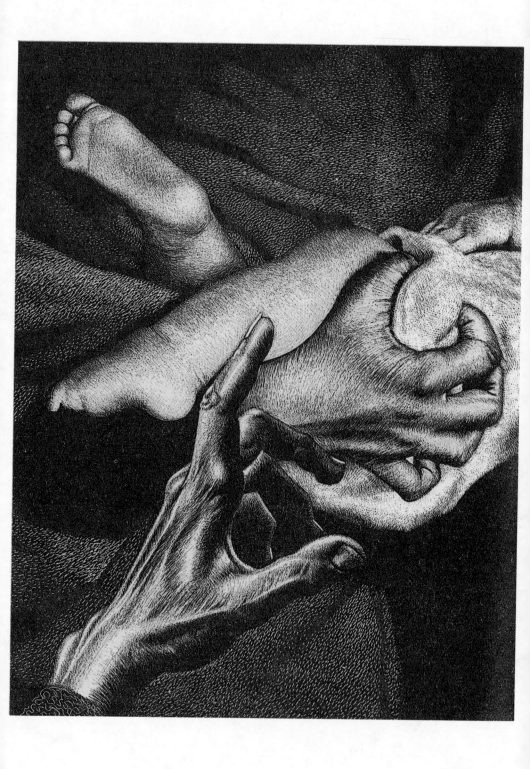

I DOLOR

The Prophecy of Simeon

THE CAUSE OF OUR JOY

WHAT contrasts in this first picture!

Not only the vivid black and white, scratched on the shallow surface; not only age and youth as they stand out in the hand of a man and the hand of a woman; not only the beginning of life as seen in the Child, and the end of life as noted in the presence of the Prophet; but the deep, deep truths of God and man, the endless forgetfulness of one, and the eternal mindfulness of the Other; love's condescension in sharp contrast to the beloved's disdain. All are there—life and death, joy and sorrow, pain and perfect bliss.

At first glance one catches only the aged hand of a man lifted in warning, pointing to the heart of a woman who clutches the white body of her child closer to her breast. But these drawings were not made for a first glance only. They are to be studied. They hold messages that are most personal and lessons that will last as long as God.

Do you see yourself in this picture? You are there! Each line is drawn in such a way that it has final focus in you. If you do not see yourself, the trouble is not with your eyes. It is not myopia. It is the amnesia already mentioned. Your memory must stir. Your mind must awake. Then you will see aright. In these few lines, so skillfully scratched, one can read the Old Testament and the New; one can find the long history of God's way with men and man's way with God; the whole sad story of sin and the almost unbelievable epic of salvation. Your own life's story lies in these few lines.

As you look, and keep on looking, you will hear words that many call the loneliest words of our language. That uplifted hand of the Prophet speaks of pain, suffering, sorrow, death. The clutching hand of Mary tells of poverty, loneliness, contradiction, frustration, failure. The white body of the Child proclaims the sharp point of a sword which His Mother's heart will scabbard and the blunter point of nails His own hands and feet will hold.

I am not reading into the picture. All I say is there. You will see it if you keep on looking. You will hear it if you keep on listening. And you will learn the greatest lessons for life and proper living. For each of us is going to meet everything that has been mentioned. Who of us has not already met failure, frustration, contradiction? Who of us has not known loneliness, pain, and sorrow? Who of us is to escape death? As for poverty who is there among us who can call himself rich in the possessions of the soul, the only possessions man can keep? As for the sword and the nails... *You are His member. She is your Mother.*

This is the Way....

It teaches as its first lesson that death can be met with a happy song. Like Simeon we can cry: *Nunc dimittis*—"Now, now, O God, thou canst dismiss thy servant in peace." Sorrow and suffering can be greeted with gladness; pain saluted with a lyric poem. Like Mary we can sing: *Magnificat anima mea Dominum*—"O, yes, my soul doth magnify the Lord." As for poverty—material and spiritual—it can be bliss. *He* said so. "Blessed are the poor." And we learn in this first step on the way that old age, widowhood, loneliness in life can each be made lovely. All we have to do in life and at death is what we see the hand of Mary doing in this picture: clasp the Christ to our heart.

This is the Way—there is no other.

But we forget so much!

Would that all the old and the aging would think long **FOR** on Simeon and Anna. It is distressing to see men and **THE** women fade with their physical powers. It is wrong. It **AGING** should never be. Cardinal Newman did claim that the soul grew old with the body. But the soul, which is where the real self dwells, should grow old as fruit grows old; the soul should mellow! And why not? Life's fitful fever has been broken; the gnawing ambitions have either been satisfied or flung away; youth's craving curiosity has been curbed; sense of values sharpened; spirit of adventure channeled on the only adventure worthy of the spirit: the quest for God. The older men and women grow, the happier they should become; for there is room for elation of the spirit only, none for depression—if the soul has matured. For life is what Simeon and Anna made it: a divine romance with each human as the beloved and God Almighty as the "tremendous Lover." Each new day is another trysting time, and the place of the tryst is in your heart! But how many have forgotten. How many yet forget!

Why don't our "old men see visions, and our young men dream dreams"? Because we have been so busy about so many things, we have forgotten the one thing necessary. Old age should find us facing the west and even the deepening twilight with eyes sparkling, faces aglow, hearts beating steady and high as, like Simeon, we keep "looking for the consolation of Israel" (Lk. 2:25) or like Anna we never leave the temple, "worshipping with fastings and prayers night and day" (Lk. 2:37). Remember you are the Temple of the Holy Ghost; that God is within you; that each dawn can be greeted with the cry *"Haec est dies quam fecit Dominus*—This is the day the Lord hath made!" Yes, He has made it just for you. He has blown the sun to flame that you might know warmth and see loveliness. He has arched the sky and made it blue just for you. Greet the day with that cry: *Haec est dies quam fecit Dominus*, then go on with the resolution: "*exultemus et laetemur in ea*—let us rejoice and be glad throughout its length!" Try it for a day. You will continue it for a week. You will make it the habit of your life. Then your old age will be what God meant it to be: the happiest hours of your existence, because most filled with Him and His loving presence.

We slow up physically. Arteries harden. Joints stiffen. The step loses its spring. But that is only the animal part of us. We may slow up even mentally. The powers of perception will dull. The ability to concentrate lessen. The agility with which we leap from premise to conclusion, from thought to thought, will leave us. The memory will not be as sure. The intellect not as sharp. But there is a deeper depth to us than intellect and memory. It is our will, the deepest depth which makes us man, and that, in its focus on God, need never waver.

Active men and active women fear the onset of age; for they dread inactivity. But they are mistaken in their dread. Old age is not a time for inactivity; though it should be a time for leisure. But that leisure is to be employed in the only business of life—the business of love. That is the one business in which none of us need fail. The older we grow the more successful should we become. But for love we need leisure. That is the beauty and the bounty of age, especially a "ripe old age," one that is fully matured.

Most commentators speak of Simeon as an old man. That is not found in the text explicitly. The fact that he was so ready to die after seeing the Lord has led to this interpretation. Nevertheless he could have been a relatively young man and still glad to die after the vision granted him. But concerning Anna there can be no doubt. "She was of great age," says the Scripture, "having lived with her husband seven years from her maidenhood, and by herself as a widow to eighty-four years" (Lk. 2:36,37). That makes her at least 100 years old, unless you will have her married in very early childhood. Let us allow that both were old; that both had lost physical strength and bodily agility. Is there any sign of depression, bitterness, self-pity in their lines or their lives as we know these feelings? Not when you sing and sing that song of Simeon as we monks of Gethsemani have to sing it every Candlemas Day. As more than 250 men march up to the Abbot's throne to receive their lighted candle, that *Nunc dimittis,* with its high and happy *in pace,* with its strong, steady *lumen* and its exultant *gloria populi Tui Israel,* is repeated and repeated. The character of Simeon's soul comes out with each fresh repetition. Only a strong soul could sing what he sang. He is the wise man who learns from that song that the truer evidences of vitality for humans lie in their mind, heart, will, rather than in any bodily powers or physical strength; and that these spiritual faculties can go on developing unto the very threshold of Eternity. Simeon tells us that Browning's Rabbi Ben Ezra was right and that we all can take courage from his words:

> Grow old along with me!
> The best is yet to be,
> The last of life, for which the first was made.
>
> Our times are in His hand
> Who saith, "A whole I planned,
> Youth shows but half;
>   trust God: see all, nor be afraid!"

I have heard it said that "Widow is a lonely word. Just how lonely only widows know." Agreed. It is a lonely word. Yet Anna, at the close of her 84 years of widowhood, tells all how loneliness can be filled with a Presence and made anything but lonely. Coming up as she does at the very hour Simeon speaks his prophecy, she makes one think of the lines of Chesterton, which fashion for us a formula for living in wondrous expectancy:

> I ride forever seeking after God.
> My hair grows whiter than my thistle plume
> And all my limbs are loose; but in my eyes,
>
> The star of an unconquerable praise;
> For in my soul one hope forever sings:
> That at the next white corner of the road
> My eyes may look on Him....[5]

This picture of the past stirs memories of the almost immediate present; for this—scene in the Temple, forty days after the birth of Christ, is repeated in symbol by the liturgy every year, though we are almost two thousand years from His death. Candlemas Day is rich with symbolism. If we can read the signs aright all our days will be wealthy with the wealth of truth that gives peace to mind, strength to soul, happiness to heart.

CANDLE FLAME   The liturgy lights candles three times in your life, and each time the significance is staggering. At your baptism a candle was lighted and the priest said to you: "Receive this burning light, and without fail be true to thy baptism; keep the commandments of God, that when our Lord comes to claim His own, thou mayest be worthy to greet Him with all the saints in the heavenly court, and live forever and ever. Amen."

"Receive this burning light..." What did it all mean? What does a child or an adult want with a burning light?

That light was only a symbol. But the reality it symbolized staggers the mind. It symbolized Life—divine Life—the life of God—the life of Christ—which had just been infused into your soul by God the Holy Ghost working through the sacrament. The lovely tenuousness of the flame, wavering in silence at the wax's slender tip, told eloquently of the caution you would need all the days of

---

[5] From "The Wild Knight." *The Wild Knight and Other Poems* (New York: E. P. Dutton & Co., Inc.).

your earthly exile; for it was evident to all that the exquisite beauty in that little burst of gold with its base of blue could be blown out with the slightest breath. Had you been conscious that you were carrying the Christ-life within you as you walked a world from whose four corners came winds that sought to extinguish that flame, would you not have been more cautious? If you had but remembered the symbol of that lighted candle?

Yet, it should not have been so difficult to keep it in mind! For every Candlemas Day the liturgy recalled it for you as Holy Mother Church had her priests bless, light, and distribute this symbol of Christ. This ceremony which speaks with such clarity should have had you doing what Mary does in this picture—clasping the Christ closer to your heart! For it tells you with its gracious gesture of handing you the lighted candle just what your function is in this world. You, like Mary, are to *mother* Christ.

The figure is not mine. It comes from a Cistercian of the Golden Age. Guerric, Abbot of Igny, in France, made this sharing of the maternity of Mary the focus of the lives of his monks. He told them plainly that it is only by participating in this maternity that one reaches the fullness of the Christian life. He had them cultivate an attitude of soul which is portrayed for you in all its grandeur every time you see a mother with her newborn child. She is all solicitude for that child. So should the Christian be for the Christ Child living within him. Baptism was a birth—another Christmas Day; for it was the birth of God within the soul of the baptized. Candles and Candlemas Day have deep, moving, sublime meaning for all Christians who use their memories and their minds. They say we are to "mother" Jesus!

Does not that awaken echoes of the vibrantly virile Apostle of the Gentiles? Did not St. Paul use the same idea when in a startling metaphor he said to his beloved Galatians: "My little children, of whom I am in labor again..."Monsignor Knox's translation of the passage differs from the Douay. He has: "My little children, with whom I am again in pains as of childbirth, until Christ be formed in you" (Gal. 4:19).

That is the one life's work of every Christian: that Christ be formed in us! The Christ-life, given us at baptism was to be nourished as a mother nourishes her child, was to grow as a child grows, until it reached the full stature of the God-Man. That concept of sanctifying grace is one which will develop a proper *Christ-consciousness* in each of us, and this, in its turn, will bring us to a true and correct self-consciousness. No need, then, to "build up the ego" as the psychologists phrase it, in the man or woman who knows his or her individual worth in Christ Jesus, and his or her individual importance as Jesus Christ. The phrase is not too bold. It is theologically sound and philosophically accurate. We are His members! But members belong to a Body, and the Body with its actions belongs to the Person. Are we not right when as we look at this picture we say: "*Mary* is holding the infant Jesus"? Yet, in actual fact, it is her *hands* that hold Him, the members of her body! So, with regard to ourselves: if we be members of the Body of Christ, we are, in a very certain and true sense, *Christ*.

That brings us to a truth that needs stressing for all the aged, crippled, and underprivileged of the world; for all who are physically, mentally, socially, or economically handicapped; for all who are made to feel unwanted, useless or "in the way." It is a lesson I learned unforgettably as I watched a ninety-two year old lay brother spend years in bed, doing nothing more, it would seem, than exist. He ate a little, he slept a lot. He spoke almost never. As the weeks grew into months, and the months became years, I asked myself what he was doing on earth for self, neighbor, or God.

The answer came when I remembered that *In all God's*

great creation, there is no such thing as a useless human being!

That old lay brother was glorifying God with every breath he drew, and helping Christ complete His Passion with every exhalation. If that be not true, God is not God, and Infinite Wisdom had gone witless. For to keep that old brother breathing, God had to exert as much power as He did when He created the world. Continued existence calls for continuous creation. Hence, that brother's every breath was an act of obedience to God's *Fiat* which had brought him into being.

To obey God is to adore Him; to adore Him is to love Him; to love Him is to give Him glory.

Human life has been likened very aptly to an organ note. It continues to sound only as long as the one at the console keeps his finger on the key. God is at the console of humanity; His fingers are on the keys! So long as we live, it follows that God has purpose for our particular note in the piece He would play. We, the smallest of us, are important to God. Without us there would be a flaw in the harmony of the concert which is the universe.

Further, we are His members—members of the Man who would save all men. He redeemed all by obedience to the Father. We, by mere existence, offer to that same Father an Act of Obedience. If we are *in Christ Jesus,* that mere Act can be of incalculable value for the entire world. That is why there is no such thing as a useless human being in God's great world; for while there is life, there is not only hope, there is faith and charity and glory to God!

The last time a candle will be kindled near you, is the time men call death. But by having that golden flower burst into beauty at the wax's tip the Church is telling men that death is not what they take it to be. In the liturgy light is always a symbol of life. And at this solemn moment it is a symbol of that life which He won for us who said of Himself: "I am the resurrection and the life; he who believes in me, even if he die, shall live; and whoever lives and believes in me, shall never die" (Jn. 11:25, 26). That is why the priest sings in every Requiem Mass: *Vita mutatur, non tollitur.* Life goes on. Life is changed; it is not taken away. The candle burns by the body, a symbol that the soul never dies. If we would only remember that "every death is a resurrection" then with Simeon we would sing: *Nunc dimittis...*

Let every candle remind us of the divine Life we received at baptism, the Christ-life we nourish all the day long, and the life immortal to which we go. Then, like Leon Bloy, if we are asked at our last hour what we feel, we will answer as he did "A keen curiosity." We will improve on that answer and say "Love's impatience!" Yes, we will be impatient to see our Mother. Death alone can grant us that vision.

"But," it has been said, "it is not death men fear; it is what comes after. We all know we are to live on. And there is the rub. After this life, comes the judgment."

There precisely is where Mary comes in—and comes in as our Mother!

Another of those wise old Cistercians of the Middle Ages, Adam of Perseigne, said to his monks: "With what *confidence* we should be led to God through Mary! For Mary, thou art the Mother of the exiled and the Mother of their King; the Mother of the accused and the Mother of their judge; the Mother of man and the Mother of God. Through you, Mother Mary, we, the accused, have been made brothers of the judge."

Would you be afraid to be judged by your own brother who loved you so much he willingly offered his life for you? That is the reality hinted at in this drawing, which shows Jesus at the moment of His Presentation to God the Father. In a certain sense this was the "Offertory" of His Mass—the Mass that was offered for us.

In preaching confidence to his monks because of their Mother, Adam of Perseigne was but following a family tra-

dition. St. Bernard, most well known of all Cistercian
fathers, preached little else. In one sermon on the birthday
of our Blessed Virgin Mother he said to the monks of
Clairvaux: "You were afraid to approach the Father...so He
gave you Jesus as your mediator. Mary has given Him to
you as your Brother. But, perhaps, you fear even Jesus; for
in Him there is Divine Majesty since, although He became
Man, He, nevertheless, remained God. Do you wish to
have an Advocate with Him? Turn to Mary!...The Son
will hear His Mother; and the Father will hear the Son.
My little children, this is the ladder for sinners. This is my
greatest confidence. This, the whole reason for my hope."[6]

We busy people in this hurried, noisy century never
take time enough to think on the deep things of God and
the only important things of man. How many of us realize vividly just how much we mean to Mary, the Mother
of Christ, and how much the Mother of Christ means to
us Christians? Adam of Perseigne said, "It is only through
her that we can find our way back to God." And again,
"Salvation is the reward of those who find Mary." Those
statements ought to make us pause.

As you look now at the picture John Andrews has
drawn, hear Blessed Guerric of Igny say: "She gave birth to
the only Son of God, and it is the same only Son whom
she now embraces in all His members." Look, and feel the
pressure of Mary's hand upon *yourself!*

Do you begin to see why I have said that every line in
this picture converges and rests finally on you? You are
Simeon "looking for the consolation of Israel"; you are
Mary ever mothering Jesus; you are His member, and
hence, can be called the Christ! Oh, if we were only conscious at all times of how dear we are to Christ and His
Mother, and how near Christ and His Mother are to us life
would be the divine Romance God meant it to be!

Look again at that white hand and what it holds; for **DREAMS**
this picture is not only for the aged and those whose sun **COME TRUE**

---

[6]   Serm. Nativ. BVM:7.

of life is far in the west. It is for those also whose sun is at aurora and the dawn. Mary was young. Jesus just forty days old. That is why there are lessons not only for the aged, the widowed, and the lonely, but for the married and unmarried, those just beginning conjugal life and those just beginning earthly life.

To the newlyweds this hand of Mary is saying: "Obedience to law is the greatest liberty; conformity to the Will of God the secret of unalloyed happiness." How our newlyweds need that lesson! How they need every lesson of this picture and the mystery it portrays.

Let them look long at the picture and find not only themselves in every line, but also the unportrayed virgin-husband and virgin-father, the great St. Joseph! Hidden saint that he was, he appears but vaguely in the gospel narrative under that inclusive plural "they" and is seen in this drawing only by those who know what is portrayed. He is there; for it was he who purchased the two turtle doves, "the offering of the poor"—it was he who presented the birds, one for Purification of his immaculate spouse, one for thanksgiving to God for the Child; and it was he who paid the five shekels to ransom the Son of God back from the service of God! All contradictions, are they not? Mary needed no purification. Jesus needed no Presentation. Joseph needed to pay no ransom. But there was the law of God. They would give a lesson to all who would live happily: follow the law of God no matter how "reasonable" may seem the reasons for not doing so!

Is not the answer to what is wrong with marriage today here in the action of Joseph and Mary? When God's law is obeyed, there is not only order in life, there is the "tranquillity of order" which Augustine called "peace"; there is joy—a thing far different from mere pleasure!

If you want joy, Joseph says, be all trust. If there is room in a man's heart for the slightest shadow of suspicion, for single shred of doubt, he does not yet love his

woman with all his heart. The thrill that came to Joseph as
he stood there in the Temple listening to Simeon sing and
Anna praise God is one that would have him say to all
young husbands: "Believe your dreams! They will come
true!"

In a chapter called "The Recovery of Love"[7] Fr. Gerald
Vann, O.P., has a passage that seems a description of
Joseph as he stands here watching Mary clasp Jesus the
tighter. Fr. Vann had been talking about the liturgy of the
marriage ceremony, he pauses on the line which the man
speaks to the woman: "With my body I thee worship..."
and says it really means: "I approach thee with wonder and
awe and tenderness and humility, for 'Thou' is a mystery,
and love is a mystery, and human sex is a mystery, and the
body is a mystery; and so they all have to be learned slow-
ly, gradually, lovingly, patiently, humbly, like a poem or a
symphony; and it is *thee* I worship with my body, the real
person, this human being with these faults and weaknesses, these poverties and needs; and so here, and there, and
again, I will try to say 'Not my will, but thine be done';
and so, out of the darkness the discovery will come."

Of course we know that Mary was without "faults and
weaknesses"—but the "poverties and needs" were real
enough; and so was the "darkness" out of which Joseph
had to make his "discovery." Here in the Temple, when a
Prophet and a Prophetess came forward to proclaim the
forty-day-old Child as "the light of revelation to the
Gentiles and a glory for the people of God, Israel," Joseph
knew that dreams come true! And Mary...

We must never forget that what was the first dolor on
the *Via Matris* was the fourth of Mary's joyful Mysteries.
It is true that her heart was pointed to and proclaimed a
future scabbard for a sword, but as she stood there in the
Temple and heard her Son proclaimed the Saviour and had
her husband listen to human beings recognizing her Child
as all that the Angel had told Joseph in sleep He would be,

---

7   From *The Water and the Fire* (New York: Sheed and Ward, 1953).

that heart filled with rarest joy. Indeed, dreams come true—for all who are faithful.

Mary and Joseph have a further lesson for moderns, more joy filling than any yet. They tell young couples how sublimely sacred marriage is. They tell them that the fruit of their dedicated loves can be *Christ!* They tell them that in procreation husband and wife are "ministers of God's omnipotence"; they prepare syllables God can make into His Word! They set out the flint from which God can strike sparks for the Light of the World. How ineffably sacred is human love when expressed in God's Great Sacrament! Let every Catholic mother realize that, when she holds her baptized child in her arms, John Andrews could use her for a model—she is Mary in the modern world; she is holding Christ.

"FEAR NOT" But the pointing finger and the clutching hand speak of something else that fills our day—and should fill the heart of every Christian with joy. Simeon's prophecy is being fulfilled before our eyes. Mary's Son is being contradicted. But by God's great mercy we are among those who rise because of Christ. We rise above all fear of those who would make a god of man, a paradise of earth, and a religion out of a false philosophy.

Why should we fear? They who have perfected techniques to take the mind from man can go only as far as the lance of Longinus went Good Friday afternoon. He touched the heart of God with steel. But he never reached His soul! Sunday morning the soul came back to the body that had been crucified and the heart that had been broken, and other Roman soldiers had reason to say: "Indeed this was the Son of God!" Essentially the techniques of the Communists do not differ from those used by the Caesars. And the Garden of Nero, the sands of the Roman arena and the broken arches of the Colosseum ought to tell the modern Caesars they are striving to kill that which cannot die, just as the crypts in the catacombs and the dome of St.

Peter's ought to tell us Christians what the angels told shepherds the night He was born, and what He told Magdalen and the Holy Women the day He rose from the dead: "Fear not!"

How that imperative runs through the whole history of our Faith! Gabriel spoke it to Mary at the Annunciation: "Fear not, Mary..." Christ spoke it again and again to the Apostles during His Public Life, and in apparition after apparition of His glorified Self the first words are: "Fear not—it is I!"

How salutary it is to remember that we can lose our minds without ever losing our souls, to recall what Christ said about him "who loses his life for my sake," and His explicit charge: "do not be afraid of those who kill the body but cannot kill the soul. But rather be afraid of him who is able to destroy both soul and body in hell" (Mt. 10:28). That whole section of Matthew's tenth chapter, wherein Christ uses the words "do not be afraid" three distinct times within six short verses, is well worth meditative reading in these days when Simeon's prophecy is being so savagely fulfilled.

The prospect before us is not pleasant. Yet it is glorious! Pius XI said we face the darkest hour since the Deluge. Yet his description was left incomplete, perhaps purposefully. This darkest hour since the Deluge is the brightest since the first Easter dawn; for never is Christian more Christly than when on the cross!

Leon Bloy was once asked what he was bringing his children up to be. Like a flash that Christian genius replied: "To be martyrs!" What more glorious career could a parent desire for his child? Was it Pascal who said "there are only two actions that fully befit man: adoration and martyrdom"?

The prospect before Mary after this prophecy by Simeon was not pleasant, but how did she face it? We are told in Luke's second chapter. The silences of Scripture are so eloquent. What poise and peace, what utter fearlessness and supreme fortitude are found in those dignified lines: "And when they had fulfilled all things as prescribed in the law of the Lord, they returned into Galilee, to their own town of Nazareth" (Lk. 2:39). Those words are as pregnant with meaning as "There stood by the Cross of Jesus, his mother" (Jn. 19:25).

This was the first step on "The Way"—she took it as He took His final ones toward the Holy City for that "baptism wherewith He would be baptized and for which He was straitened until it be accomplished." There was joy in His step and there was joy in hers; for nothing in all the world can give joy to the heart like doing the will of God. Christ sings but once in the Gospels; it is on the night He rises from table, from what was His Last Supper, to go out into the Garden and to His death. Mary sings aloud but once in the Gospels; it was after Elizabeth greeted her as "Mother of God." Her song was the *Magnificat*. You can be sure that as she left the Temple this day of Purification and Presentation her heart was singing, and again it was the *Magnificat anima mea Dominum*. For indeed God had made her great, had added another dignity to that of being the Mother of His Son. By turning her heart into a scabbard, God had made her Co-Redemptress of the world. Do you see why the prospect was glorious? She had just been granted the greatest share possible in the work of Jesus Christ. And you, if Simeon's prophecy should be filled out in you, would you not sing *Magnificat anima mea Dominum?* You would be sharing closely in the salvation of mankind; you would be "filling up those things that are wanting to His Passion"; you would be living out your baptism in all its glory; you would be truly His member. You would be Christ.

Remember your dignity and you will never know fear. You are a candle flame of the Light of the World. Let your light shine in the darkness of a world turned pagan, and though the darkness comprehend it not, God and His Mother will! Remember that Our Lady of Light said at Fatima: "In the end My Heart shall triumph."

Remember always that you are being hugged to the Immaculate Heart of Our Lady of Light as closely as is the Christ in this drawing. She has to hold us thus; for *we are His members* and *she is our Mother!*

How often God the Holy Ghost has told us that there is joy in suffering! When Peter and the Apostles were first scourged by the Sanhedrin they departed from the presence of that Sanhedrin "rejoicing that they had been counted worthy to suffer disgrace for the name of Jesus" (Acts 5:41). Paul exultingly states: "I rejoice in the sufferings I bear for your sake" (Col. 1:24). And in that incomparable Sermon on the Mount did not Christ Himself tell us: "Blessed shall you be when men hate you, and when they shut you out, and reproach you, and reject your name as evil, because of the Son of Man"? (Lk. 6:22.)

Simeon's prophecy is being fulfilled. Therefore rejoice! Clasp Christ to your heart as tightly as Mary in this picture and you will not be afraid. Let Mary clasp Christ in you, and you in Christ, just as tightly and you will learn how she is the cause of our joy and how the first step on the *Via Matris* is a giant stride *ad Patrem, Patriam et Patrimonium;* a giant stride "toward our heritage, our home, and our heavenly Father!"

This is the Way; there is no other!

II DOLOR

The Flight Into Egypt

CONSOLATION FOR THE AFFLICTED

WHAT does the Flight into Egypt—something that happened twenty centuries ago—mean to men and women who have never crossed a desert, never ridden a plodding donkey, never clasped a child in protecting arms?

What significance does the title: "Flight into Egypt" have for moderns? What sounds do they hear; what sights do they see, as they gaze at this artistic representation of the Second Step in *The Way?*

Most moderns would find it meaningless, I fear. Yet in the hands of this Woman is the only thread that will ever lead us out of the labyrinth we ourselves have constructed, and in which we are lost. Greek mythology tells of Ariadne, the daughter of the King, who saved the hero she loved by giving him a thread which led him out of the complex cave wherein the Minotaur dwelt and devoured the men and maidens who entered there. The beauty of Ariadne, the bravery of Theseus, the labyrinth itself are all mere fiction. But Mary, the Child, the modern labyrinth and the deaths of men and maidens therein are anything but myth. We need what Mary holds in her hands—all of us.

History is ever repeating itself. Today we speak of "displaced persons." They are people who are in flight just as Mary was, and "Egypt" is their goal. We have seen pictures of many children who had been evacuated from homes and countries destroyed by war. But how many of us saw in those pictures what John Andrews has scratched for us in this one?

Caryll Houselander tells of a Bavarian peasant woman who had lost her only son in World War I. He had been everything to her. So neighbors were surprised when they learned that she had adopted another son. They were more surprised to find that he was just the opposite to the one the peasant woman had lost. Her son had been blue-eyed, golden haired, fair complexioned. The son she now had was a Negro. Yet on him she lavished all the love she had on the child of her womb. When one neighbor grew bold enough to say: "I never thought you would allow anyone to take the place of your dead child," this wise peasant woman replied: "I haven't. There is only one Child in all the world—He is the Christ."

Moderns may sneer at her, and at me, as they exclaim: "From myth to mysticism in less than a page!" But it is just such sneering that has built the labyrinth, put them in there, and buries them ever deeper in its depths. Mysticism is highest realism. It is the modern who has lost touch with reality. It is the modern who is blind and deaf. They have "eyes and see not; ears and hear not." It was of such that Thompson wrote: "'Tis ye, 'tis your estranged faces, that miss the many-splendoured thing."

If God be Truth, and the Bible the Word of God, the peasant woman was most right: there is only one Child in all the world; He is the Christ. For did not Jesus sunder the heavens years after His Ascension and cry to Saul: "Why persecutest thou me?"—Saul was persecuting Christians; it was Christ who called out. The same Christ who at the Last Supper had said: "I am the Vine, you are the branches." The same Christ of whom we say: He is the Head of the Body, and we are His members! That fifth verse in the ninth chapter of the Acts of the Apostles has

more—power, more dynamism, more might than anything yet discovered or invented by atomic fission experts.
When the blinded Saul looked up and asked "Who art
thou, Lord?" and received the reply, "*I am Jesus, whom
thou art persecuting,*" a greater force was let loose in the
world than anything man will ever devise. It made possible such a marvel as this Bavarian peasant woman and her
mystic remark: "There is only one Child in all the world;
He is the Christ." It made possible the joy she knew after
the desolation caused by the death of her own son. It will
go on making marvels and creating joys until our old earth
with all its atomic energy has ceased to be and all atomic
experts have learned who it was created the atom.

When I say that moderns sneer at mysticism I mean
not only confessed pagans, but also confused Christians
and some contaminated Catholics. To the tenets of our
Credo too many of us give only an assent that has been
called by Newman "notional." We believe, but it is not
with all our body and all our blood; it is not with our
whole being. It is not what the same great Cardinal called
a "real" assent. If it were, then Archbishop Cushing would
never have to rise at a crowded Communion breakfast and
say: "If the peoples of the free world are to save civilization
for Christ, they will have to acquire three characteristics
prominent among the Communists: *zeal* for the cause, a
keen *sense of solidarity* with their fellow-man, and an *undy-
ing loyalty* to the leader."

Think of it: after two thousand years of Christianity
with Christ as Leader, His Kingdom as the cause, and His
Mystical Body to give that keen sense of solidarity, we have
to learn from the false religion of the Reds! No wonder Fr.
Leo Trese has said: "The danger of the day is not
Communism, but Christian apathy."

We are apathetic because the great realities have never
taken hold on us. We are not possessed by Truth. We are
not obsessed by the realization that we are Christ. The

candle flame of our baptism flickers feebly because we do not feed the wick with the rich wax of our memory. Forgetfulness of our dignity deprives the whole world of light, and ourselves of the ecstasy of love.

The ever realistic Fr. Gillis once wrote that "any religion that is more than a system of philosophical thought, more than an interpretation of life, more than a moral code, *must* be mystical. For after all, what is religion but contact with the other world?" He went on to say that "Religion, rightly understood, is not a dull dogged prosaic uninspired manner of life, though Puritans and Pharisees and formalists have made it seem so. Religion is adventure, the kind of adventure that even the boldest *conquistadores* never dared attempt."[8]

Have you ever felt your religion to be such an adventure? If not, it is only because you have forgotten the wonder of your baptism.

Jean Mouroux in *The Meaning of Man* wrote: "When man has become Christian, he finds entrance to a new mystery. He is born a second time and of God Himself, he has become a member of Christ, possessed of eternal life, he is the temple of the Holy Spirit, 'signed upon' and consecrated even as to his body, he participates the life of the Society which links the Father, the Son, and the Spirit in the bonds of Infinite Love. Thereby he is rapt away into the holiness of God, and by this contact with the divine fire he becomes even more of a holy thing than before, because God Himself now dwells within him; because in the eyes of the Father and in reality he is indeed another Christ; because he is thus taken out of the whole order of things profane, and is destined to glorify God in his soul and in his body till the Glory Itself shall consume him forever."[9]

He ends that magnificent passage with *Agnosce, O Christiane, dignitatem tuam!* The words of St. Leo the Great, if memory serves me right. Words that mean exact-

---

[8]   From *So Near Is God* (New York: Charles Scribner's Sons, 1953), pp.178, 179.

[9]   From Frank Sheed's *The Mary Book* (New York: Sheed and Ward, 1950), p.405.

ly what I have been saying all along: "Be mindful of your dignity, you who call yourself Christian!" Remember you are to "mother" Christ. Therefore you will have to "rise, take the Child and fly into Egypt," if you are to save Him from the sword of Herod.

It is again the hand of Mary, as drawn by John Andrews, that stirs memories. We know the story well enough. We can tell it quickly and quite clearly. But have we ever understood all that that story tells?

Look at this hand of Mary clasping the Christ in love and fright—and learn that life is undulant. The words of Gabriel troubled Mary. His explanation of how the Incarnation was to take place scattered the clouds. The Visitation was sheer joy with Elizabeth adding to the "Hail Mary," Zachary singing his sublime *Benedictus,* John the Baptist dancing in his mother's womb, and under Mary's own Immaculate Heart the Sacred Heart, beating, as it were, with her own blood and timed to the tempo of her own pulse. Small wonder her soul poured forth the limpid strains of the *Magnificat.* But how soon she was in anguish as the young brow of her espoused husband furrowed in anxiety. Life is undulant even for the Mother of God! An angel smooths Joseph's brow and lifts Mary's heart. But soon the doors of Bethlehem close in their faces. "He came unto His own, and His own received Him not." But that agony was banished by the birth in the cave, the *Gloria in excelsis* of angels, and the visit of the shepherds. Then came the bittersweet visit to the Temple when praise of Jesus was followed by promise of a sword for Mary. They go home. While Mary is "pondering these things in her heart" a star leads Magi from the east. In them Mary sees fulfillment of Simeon's prophecy about Jesus being "a Light of revelation to the Gentiles." If she was wondering when the rest of his prophecy was to be fulfilled, she did not wonder long; for the Magi had hardly departed when Joseph shook her out of slumber and told that she must arise and they must fly

LIFE IS UNDULANT

at once, in the night, for Herod sought the life of the Child.

Look at this hand of Mary hugging that Child as a sea of sand stretches before them and the steel of Herod's soldiery threatens from behind and learn not only that life is undulant, but that God almost always does the unexpected. Here are the most loved persons on earth; the three dearest to God Almighty—Joseph, they say, was sanctified in his mother's womb; theologians are now arguing about him as they did about Mary centuries ago, and the argument from "fittingness" is showing Joseph in his true colors. After Mary there was no one on earth as close to Jesus nor as beloved of the Father and the Holy Ghost. Yet look at his life up to now. He won Mary's hand. They vowed virginity. Then as reward, it would seem, for this magnanimous gift to God, both Joseph's and Mary's hearts were almost broken as he found her with Child. He obeys God in Caesar. That is why he took Mary to Bethlehem. God had spoken through lawfully constituted authority. And for this generous fulfilling of a command, how did God reward him? "By allowing no room for them in the Inn!" He circumcises God and gives Him that name which is above all names. Then, in obedience to an ordinance which really did not bind them, he takes Mother and Child to the Temple only to have her Immaculate Heart smitten by the prophecy of Simeon. Magi come and adore; offer gifts to this Jewish Child. Joseph is shaken out of his sleep because the Jewish King seeks the life of Him whom Gentiles adored. No room for them in the Inn before birth; now shortly after birth, no room for them in the whole Kingdom of the Jews.

Look at this picture long and know that this is God who *is in flight!* that it is God's Mother and "the man nearest to Christ" who are *in fright!* With that in mind you will understand that strange line of Gertrud von le Fort in *Hymns to The Church:* "I will go into deepest sorrow that I may find my God!"…It is not sorrow, not sadness, not suffering that God sends His most beloved friends on earth; it is a share He grants them in the Passion of His only Son. It is the greatest gift He could bestow after creation and re-creation by baptism! It is *glory* for those who have studied the ways of God with men for those who have watched God's Mother on her "Way."

We moderns shrink from pain; we shun all that can afflict body or mind. We have forgotten that we were saved by the Body's agony and the Mind's torture. We have forgotten that the problem of evil was solved by ropes, whips, and thorns, by nails that were pounded through the flesh of God and by three hours of anguish such as no other human has or ever will know. We have forgotten that pain has a sacred purpose; that all suffering can be and should be sublimated into Sacrifice—His Sacrifice. We have forgotten that we are Christians—members of a Body whose Head is thorn-crowned! We have forgotten that since there is sin, there must be suffering that will atone.

Those are some of the memories that will aid our mind to understand why it is that God is in flight and His parents in fright. Is it not clear now that there are but two realities on earth: Sin and Salvation? Christ and Herod? Those who face the desert and those who slaughter innocents?

This picture is for today. Herod's sword has never known scabbard since that Idumean monster unsheathed it by his command "to massacre all the male children in Bethlehem who were two years of age or under." But the tragedy of our times is that too often his steel touches the Christ! The fault is with us Christians. We are not like Joseph. We do not believe in dreams that manifestly come from God. We are not like Mary. We do not believe that God could speak to us through mere mortals, especially by one who says he learned God's will in his sleep! No, we do not believe—and Christ dies very young!

We must fly into Egypt with the Christ in our arms. We must fly often! For the soldiers of Herod are many and their swords are sharp. Mary was a Virgin—how is virginity viewed in the world of today? Caryll Houselander tells me "There is nothing so little appreciated by the world today as purity; nothing so misunderstood as virginity." She tells me further that "in many minds virginity is associated with negative qualities, with impotence"—Let them look at the Virgin of all virgins and realize that never was woman more woman than when she gave her all to God out of that which makes women truly womanly—love! Virginity, far from being in any way synonymous with impotence, is more nearly related to Omnipotence. There is a "virginity" about God the Father, God the Son, and God the Holy Ghost; and of earth's holy Trinity, Jesus was a virgin, Mary was a virgin, Joseph was a virgin. Never is man more manly than when he gives his virginal all to God. For then he is being more knightly than any Galahad in Arthur's Round Table; stronger than any Samson—for he slays fiercer lions than Samson ever knew! and offers sacrifice to God more kingly than any David or Solomon gave. As for virginity being allied to sterility—Mary, the Virgin, became Mother not only of God but of all men! And today, in these United States there are 140,000 virgins who have become "mothers" to multitudes. We call them "Sisters" and "Mothers"; each of them calls herself "Mary." Without them the far-flung parochial school system, the Catholic system of higher education, the sublime work done in orphanages, homes for foundlings and for the aged, our countless Catholic hospitals and most of our social service would be at a standstill. Nothing sterile about that array of functioning, factual forces. Yet behind each is the inspiration of the Virgin of all virgins, and her mother-love for Christ.

And our youth...is there not a veritable conspiracy

against purity going on against them? Much was made of "muckraking journalism" in the early decade of this century, but was not that clean compared with what comes off the press today in tabloids, magazines, paper-backed books, and even newspapers? Look at our ads and ask yourself how are they calculated to affect youth? Yes, Christ is exposed to Herod's steel in the minds and hearts of our youth. Bethlehem is only two hours from Jerusalem. It is night. Must we not arise and flee?

This conspiracy against purity goes a step further and attacks newlyweds. The swords are sharpened by economic pressure and their points made more piercing by the wheel of pleasure. But how can our young married couples forget that God Himself when on this earth pointed to the birds of the air and the flowers of the field? How can they forget that Incarnate Truth said: "If you ask the Father anything in my name, He shall give it to you?" How can they forget that marriage is God's "Great Sacrament"— that in it they share the very power of God to bring forth new life? How can they be so forgetful of Paul's words: "Are you not aware that your body is the temple of the Holy Spirit? Him you have received from God! You are not your own masters. You have been bought, and at a price! So then, glorify God in your body" (I Cor. 6:19, 20).[10] If husband and wife have any respect for one another—I do not speak of love—they will awake to the fact that Herod has turned his soldiers loose and they had better fly in the night. It is the only way to save the Christ!

We have had better than an angel waken us in our sleep or speak to us in our dreams; we have had the Mother of God, the Queen of Angels and Archangels, come to us at LaSalette, Lourdes, Pontmain, and Fatima to tells us that though innocents are being slaughtered, it is not too late for us to save what Herod would destroy.

Does not John Andrews' picture cause you to hear the cry that was heard in Rama? Are you a modern Rachel

---

[10] Kleist-Lilly translation.

weeping for your children who should be and are not? If so, come down to Egypt and learn how exile can be heaven. These pictures of Mary's dolors are to prove the cause of joy.

"I blessed the Lord to be able to suffer these," said our Lady to Blessed Mary of Agreda. She was talking of the flight into Egypt and the exile there. It was a source of suffering and a real sorrow. For the Magi had most likely told her how Herod was intensely interested in their story and how he begged them to come back when they found the Child so that he, too, might come and adore. Mary might have thought that since Jesus was shining as "a light of revelation to the Gentiles" as Simeon had said, He would also be "a glory for Israel" at this time, too. Think of what it would have meant to Herod and all Israel if that greedy, jealous creature had harkened to grace in the persons of the Magi and the shining of their star. Think what a different ending there would have been to his life—and to their history. And learn that grace is never to be trifled with! So it must have come as a shock to Mary to be aroused as she was, and made to flee.

It is good to know that the way down to the desert was no highway. It was nothing but a steep path that had been trodden by man and beast for centuries. Mary and Joseph had to traverse part of it by night. Jerusalem was only two hours away. They could not spare a split second. It was a night of terror for both. In the morning they were in the land of the Philistines. Another full day brought them to Gaza, the last city before they embarked on that sea of sand. These two days and nights had been filled with dread. Every hoof beat of a donkey behind them had Mary clasping the Child closer and Joseph looking anxiously at the oncoming beast and its rider. Every face that appeared suddenly from behind a vineyard wall gave them a start. Herod's arm could reach them still! Whenever a chance passer-by happened to look a bit intently at the Mother and Child Joseph felt a chill round his heart, and Mary hugged Jesus closer to her breast.

Then came that yellow sand. Far to the west it rose in dunes and blotted out some of the low horizon. Beyond the dunes lay the sea. Spurred by the urgency in the angel's voice Joseph hurried on, striving to steer a straight path between the dunes on one side with their drifts and deep sand which made travel slow and difficult, and the flatter desert on the other, where one could so easily lose direction.

Every step of the way in this desert brought fresh memories to Mary. Abraham, father of Israel, had come through it. Joseph, after whom her spouse was named, had been taken across it, as Jesus was now, with the same foreign land as his destination. Joseph's brothers had come when famine gripped all the land. He sent them back for Benjamin, and finally for Jacob. Mary was now carrying Him whom the God of Abraham, Isaac, and Jacob had promised as a Saviour for His People. These were the sands Moses and the Chosen People trod when God led them out of exile. Now she was taking God into exile. What good reasons she had for "pondering these things in her heart" and marveling at the strange ways of God and the undulancy of life!

At last they are in Egypt, and dread leaves them, for the angel had implied that safety awaited them here.

But what loneliness also awaited them! There were Jews in Egypt. To some ghetto Joseph took Mary and the Child. But fellow countrymen are not always neighbors. A man who has been brought up in a small country parish and has known the intimacy of pastor and flock is lost and very lonely when he moves to a large city parish where neither pastor nor curates can tell the exact number of parishioners they have, let alone their names. Some such loneliness the Holy Family now knew.

Then the uncertainty of it all. The Angel had said, "Be

there until I give thee further notice." Would that be days, months, or years?

Finally the surroundings of the present and the associations of the past all made for pain. This was a land of idols. How it hurt Mary to nurse Jesus at her breast while some Egyptian worshiped a snake or crocodile before her eyes! She saw slaves making bricks and had to think of the straw that was denied her ancestors by the Pharaohs, who yet demanded the bricks. The Pyramids silhouetted against a burning blue sky could not but make her think of the "Kings who knew not Joseph" and the oppression of her people. The red waters of the Nile reminded her of the days when every male child born of the Jews was supposed to be slaughtered. And she hugged Jesus closer. Those waters made her think of Moses and the Paschal Lamb; how doorposts were marked with that lamb's blood so that life would be spared to those within. And she hugged Jesus closer. Here was a Leader and Liberator greater than Moses; here was the true Paschal Lamb whose blood would save a world. But she must save Him. Whenever an Egyptian woman would show interest in the Child and, as is the wont with women, ask His name, Mary would smile and say "Jesus"—and all the marvel, the ecstasy of the Annunciation would come back to her. But when the Egyptian would frown and say: "What a strange name for a child!" Mary would remember the words of Simeon.

There was pain in Egypt—yet, I say it was heaven.

Mary saw raw, rampant paganism all about her, yet she nursed God at her breast; she had to listen to false gods being called upon, yet she heard the Word of God utter His first human word. And while the sight of pyramids standing out against a setting sun, and the shimmer on the waters of the Nile told her not only that she was in exile, but that her whole people had once been here, yet when she gazed into the starry light in His eyes and knew that it had been kindled from light in her own and that He was the Maker of the stars, Egypt and exile was heaven. It was here she saw Him take His first step, listened to Him laugh in baby glee, felt His tiny hand caress her cheek and tangle in her hair; it was here that she bathed, clothed, fed her Baby who was God; it was here that she tucked God in bed and sang God to sleep; it was here that her whole night and day, her whole being, her whole existence was God who was also her Child. If to know and love God is heaven, then to labor and live and love Jesus in Egypt is a heavenly exile.

Have you ever tried to live a whole day not only for God but with Him? We are in exile. Every night we monks sing to Mary and confess that we are *exules filii Evae*—the exiled children of Eve. But that song is a knightly tribute to our Queen and our Mother. In it we ask that she turn her eyes, so full of mercy, toward us. It has frequently struck me as a needless request. The Portuguese call Mary *Gobba* which means "hunchback." They say she is round-shouldered or hunched-back from bending out of heaven down toward her "poor banished (exiled) children of Eve." If Pascal was right when he said Jesus will be in agony until the end of the world, we are not wrong when we say Mary will be standing by His cross all the while. She is our Mother—and mothers never rest until their children are home. Mary will be *Gobba* until time ends. We need not beg her to "turn thine eyes of mercy toward us"—they are always on us. But like all mothers she likes to be asked; for she likes to know that we are conscious not only of our need, but of her ability to help.

Another phrase in that nightly *Salve* of ours I would also like to change. We cry: "After this, our exile, show unto us the blessed fruit of thy womb—Jesus." Why not ask this "omnipotent" Mother to show us Jesus now while we are in exile—and thus make our "Egypt" what hers was—a bit of heaven? She will point to our fellow human beings and say: "There is my Child!" She will remind us of the Bavarian peasant woman with her saying: "There is only one Child in all the world: He is Jesus."

TRY THIS   Wake each morning with a greeting on your lips for Jesus. Saying, "Good morning, Lord. Thank You for the night and this new day. This is the day the Lord hath made. Let us spend it together for the glory of the Father and the good of mankind," is not a bad way to begin. Don't speak to God as if He were three billion light years away! He is closer to you than the Child in Mary's arms. Remember your baptismal candlelight. Jesus is within you! Talk to yourself in the right way and you will be talking to God. That is how near God is. "Lo here! Lo there! Ah, me, lo everywhere!"

You have no difficulty about believing that Christ is present in a consecrated Host, have you? Yet you were not born with such a belief! You acquired it by using your intellect, memory, and will—elevated by grace, the virtues and the gifts. You got the habit of believing from repeated acts. Do the same now with men and women and children as you did then with Consecrated Bread and Wine. The Presence is as real, though in a different order. It is mystical not sacramental but just as real as the life of the Vine is real in the branches.

Relatively few are allowed to spend their whole day in a convent, monastery, or church. Yet no one should spend his or her day, or one hour of the day, without being consciously in the presence of God. It demands an exercise of memory. It requires an effort of mind and will. But it can become second nature to us if we are willing to pay the price: repeated acts! God is within us and within every creature. Christ is in the baptized, living in those who are in grace, dead—as He was in the tomb—in those who are in mortal sin. So we can greet Him and worship Him in all our fellow beings. Even the unbaptized are His potential members. Hence, we can find God everywhere if we will but look aright.

St. Paul was forever preaching this doctrine of the Mystical Body, and he was as conscious—as I am—that many shy from It as "too mysterious." Yet what is more simple than the analogy of the Vine and the Branches? What is more understandable than the unity of the Body with its members and head?—Paul, in his Second Epistle to the Corinthians, wrote: "Our gospel is a mystery, yes, but it is only a mystery to those who are on the road to perdition; those whose unbelieving minds have been blinded by the god this world worships, so that the glorious gospel of Christ, God's image, cannot reach them with the rays of its illumination....The same God who bade light shine out of darkness has kindled a light in our hearts, whose shining is to make known his glory as he has revealed it in the features of Jesus Christ" (II Cor. 4:3-6).[11]

Does not that remind you of the candle flame of baptism? The same God who said *Fiat lux* and darkness was dispelled, gave you the Christ light that it might shine in today's darkness! You are more than a ciborium carrying the Christ within you; you are more than a monstrance whence His whiteness might shine out; you have been made Christ—you are much more like the Host which the ciborium and the monstrance hold! "Your shining is to make known his glory *as he has revealed it in the features of Jesus Christ.*" The words are those of the Holy Ghost as He inspired St. Paul.

Our day is dark. Some predict an Age of Blackout. But has not Fr. Keller given the antidote? Is not the Chinese proverb he borrowed most applicable by the Christian. "It is better to light a candle than curse the darkness." You are the Light of the World, for again I say: You are Christ. Live not only for Him, but with Him. Do it by reminding yourself time and time again throughout the day of what Paul said to his Corinthians: "We have a treasure, then, in our keeping, but its shell is of perishable earthenware; it must be God, and not anything in ourselves, that gives it

---

[11] Knox translation.

its sovereign power...; we carry about continually in our
bodies the dying state of Jesus, so that the living power of
Jesus may be manifested in our bodies too" (II Cor.
4:7-10).[12]

Go on then to his next chapter and read what is a challenge as well as a spur: "Christ died for us all, so that being
alive should no longer mean living with our own life, but
with his life who died for us and is risen again; and therefore, henceforward, we do not think of anybody in a merely human fashion...; when a man becomes a new creature
in Christ, his old life has disappeared, everything has
become new about him" (II Cor. 5:15-17).[13] Do you see
how Paul would have you look upon yourself and upon all
other men? Do you begin to see how old this doctrine is
that I present to you? Look upon yourself and your fellow
men in no "merely human fashion" if you would see,
touch, and know reality. Since Christ came to earth, and
most especially since Christ left this earth, all things have
changed, and even exile can be heaven! It will be heaven
for all who use their memories and recall hour by hour
that we are His members.

Can you imagine what a revolution we would produce
in society, in civilization, if every one of us Catholics lived
this doctrine to the hilt twenty-four hours a day, seven
days a week, fifty-two weeks a year? What would happen
in the economic sphere? Would there be strikes such as we
have had this past decade? Would there be so many of
these superchains, these veritable monopolies? Would the
little man feel pushed to the wall and even crushed there?
Would capital and labor be like two bulls with locked
horns as they have been for so many years now? Would so
many of our fellow men be looking for principles to guide
them; would so many be deceived and led astray by false
principles, if we had *lived* the principles given by Leo XIII
in *Rerum Novarum* and by Pius XI in *Quadragesimo Anno?*
Would not the world have learned those great basic truths

---

[12] Knox translation.

[13] Knox translation.

of the dignity of man, the right to possess property, what social justice demands and what social charity asks—truths as intimately connected with economics as breath is with your heartbeat—if all Catholics had acted always on the conviction that *we* are His members; that consequently our actions are Christ's actions?

Remember now Paul's startling words about taking the members of Christ and making them the "members of a prostitute" (I Cor. 6:15); apply them in like manner to the business world. Would we have Christ either "grinding down the poor" or "soaking the rich"? Would we have Christ being in any way unjust? Would we have Him either countenancing laissez-faire capitalism or condoning those deeds which hurry us on to a centralization that looks like Socialism and has too many of the characteristics of the Slave State?

Both Leo and Pius said: "If society is to be healed now, in no way can it be healed save by a return to Christian life...." That last phrase really means: "living the life of Christ" or "living as Christ."

Need we go on to the social and political spheres? Think what it would mean to the White House and to the Kremlin; think what it would mean to your own City Council or your County judge; think what it would mean to your next-door neighbor and to your own family if you and all of us all of the time radiated the conviction that we are His members.

Remember it is not Utopia we are aiming to create; it is heaven we are trying to begin on earth. And it does begin here—or it begins not at all. But it will be only a beginning. In other words there will be sorrow, suffering, hardships of all kinds just as there were for Jesus, Mary, and Joseph in Egypt.

But they will no longer be without infinite meaning and eternal worth. Sorrow will be what Francis Thompson called it—the "Shadow of His hand outstretched caressingly." Hardships will be welcomed as St. Paul welcomed his: "I rejoice now in the sufferings I bear for your sake; and what is lacking of the sufferings of Christ I fill up in my flesh for his body, which is the Church" (Col. 1:24).

To the men and women who know what baptism has done to their being, sorrow is very like what the beatific vision is to the saints in heaven: it is the Presence of God, the manifestation of Himself, the blaze of that Light Inaccessible. A man or woman without suffering of some kind would be like a world without Divine Revelation; they would know only the twilight of God, see but dimly His vestiges and know Him almost not at all.

There *must* be suffering in this exile of ours. Else God would not be God; for He would not be just. There has been sin; therefore there will be anguish for the sinner and the sinful.

Very particularly must there be suffering for every one of us who has said "Amen" to the priest who baptized us "in the name of the Father, and of the Son, and of the Holy Ghost." To be a Christian means to become a cruci-fied. The closer we come to Christ the deeper will the nails sink and the sharper the thorns will bite. Who was closer to Christ than Mary, His Mother? Who brought suffering into the life of Mary but He who alone has physical right to call her Mother? From the moment she said *Fiat* to the angel who told her she would give birth to a Child whom she was to call Jesus, unto the moment He earned that name in all fullness by "crying out with a loud voice and giving up the ghost," Christ was a source of anguish to His Mother. It was on account of Him that Joseph doubted; it was on account of Him that Simeon prophesied; it was on account of Him that she is now in Egypt....We are to "mother" Christ; we are Christians; we will anguish, then, as Mary did! But by changing all that anguish into His Agony, we will be in heaven all the time. When your soul is crushed with sorrow, know then that it is crowded full with God.

To the little man and the little woman—and that means most of us—this step in the Way says clearly and convincingly: You are tremendously important. You hold in your hands the Wheat a starving world needs!

Psychologists say that man needs three things to be happy. He needs to feel accepted, significant, and safe. How happy, then, the member of Christ should be! For he or she has been accepted by God, is significant, tremendously significant to Jesus Christ, and is safe so long as he or she remembers that what happened to Venerable Joanna, the Franciscan nun, is symbol of his or her real life. This good Sister was praying one day when suddenly there came the noise of an angry chase. She heard the hurry of many feet, the clash of swords and clanking of arms as soldiers sped in pursuit. Looking up she saw a beautiful Boy rush toward her, fling Himself in her arms crying: "O Joanna, save me! Save me from sinners who hunt me as Herod did and would slay me."

On Holy Saturday, after the last Prophecy has been read, the priest in praying to God speaks about the prophecies having foretold the "mysteries of the present time." So you see how liturgical I have been in speaking of the Flight into Egypt being a present-day occurrence. The Incarnation of Christ goes on. He is born anew in every baptism. The Presentation takes place every day. But not enough of us fly into Egypt! That is why, after twenty centuries of miracles, from Cana with its water blushing into wine, to the Cova da Iria where the sun whirled off those splendid colors, left its place and plunged toward earth; after twenty centuries of martyrs, from Stephen to Maria Goretti, from the sands of the Arena at Rome to the stages erected behind the Iron and Bamboo curtains today; after twenty centuries of sanctity in every walk of life, from that of sovereign of realms and prime ministers, down the full gamut to poverty such as Matt Talbot practiced and

squalor such as Benedict Joseph Labre knew; after twenty
centuries of intellectual brilliance such as Augustine,
Aquinas, Bonaventure, Scotus, Suarez shed on their day,
down to a similar brilliance in a Chesterton of our own
day; after all the truth that has been poured out by the
Fathers, Doctors, ecclesiastical writers, by the twenty
Ecumenical Councils of the Church and the infallible pronouncements of our pontiffs, with the Gospels proved
authentic by the very enemies of the Church—after all
this, the world is as pagan today as when Christ was born
and had to flee. Perhaps more so! Yes, we are in Egypt: the
Pyramids stand on the edge of the desert, the Nile flows
through every land on earth—and idols are worshiped.
God, in His world today, is as hidden to most people as
He was when in Egypt's exile.

There lies the thrill for the loving soul! In this day,
when our world seems to be slipping back to the cruelty
and lust that marked the last days of the Greco-Roman
culture, we can do for Christ exactly what His Mother did
for Him when Herod sought His life. We can shelter Him
and see that He grows straight and strong within our souls,
and then let Him radiate out to all others.

When Mary looked out on the desert from her place
of refuge she must have thought of the manna that had
fallen there to feed God's Chosen People. When she
looked about her in Egypt, how could she fail to think of
Joseph the Provider—namesake of her husband, symbol
and figure of her Son—and remember how he stored corn
for a world that was to know famine. Then she breathed
deeply and realized that she was not only like Joseph, but
to an extent even somewhat like God—for she had in her
care the Wheat of all the World, the only Wine of everlasting life, the Manna for all men.

If we imitate Mary and fly into Egypt whenever Herod
seeks the life of the Child as it exists within us, whether
that seeking be with the swords of the seven capital sins

that are scabbarded in our very being, or by that almost unconquerable triple entente of the world, the flesh, and the devil, or with the double-edged sword of passion and pleasure, we will have manna every morning to strengthen us, and wine whenever we are weary; we will have heaven on earth; we will be souls brimming over with joy even while in exile.

Cultivate the consciousness that you carry Christ in your body, as Paul put it; let Him be a Child who needs protection; love will come easier and life prove more romantic. With Him in our hearts, who or what can keep them from beating high? There is no darkness when we hold the Light of the World. There is no danger when we have the Saviour. There is really no sorrow when we recall that we are His members. We will still dwell in Egypt, but the Nile will take on the tinge of the waters that gladdened Eden.

III DOLOR

The Loss of the Child

REFUGE FOR ALL SINNERS

HOLY WEEK moves on. As we live it with Christ and His
Mother, the parallel between these two Ways becomes
more striking. Sunday we took palms from our Abbot's
hands just as we took candles on the Feast of the
Presentation. Jesus went into the Temple this day; He had
been carried there that day. No Simeon or Anna come forward. Instead He drives out the buyers and sellers.
Remembering, however, that His Mother had purchased
turtle doves for her Purification He is more gentle with the
men who hover about their cages. This Sunday is very like
that Day of Candles: it is brimmed with joy and sorrow; it
is bittersweet for Him now just as that had been for her
then. There was triumph in His entry, but He spoke of
tragedy as He went back to Bethany. The pattern that had
been cut by God for His Mother serves for His and her
Son. She had known ecstasy as she went into the Temple
that day and had Him recognized and proclaimed as
"Light for Gentiles and Glory for the Jews" but a sword
was in her heart as she took Him home in her arms.

Monday He fled the City—and for much the same
reason she had carried Him off some thirty-three years ear-
lier. Herod, of course, was dead; but there were others who
"sought the life of the Child"—and His hour had not yet
come.

Now we come to a dolor that even more perfectly parallels His Way and shows that parallel lines can meet. He knew three hours of darkness. She knew three days. He cried: "My God! My God! Why hast thou forsaken me?" From a broken heart His Mother anticipated that cry by over two decades of years—and with seemingly more reason. For three days and three nights she sobbed her *Eli! Eli! lema sabacthani?*

This is the deepest mystery of Jesus' three and thirty years—this desertion of His Mother and His foster father, this fulfilling of Simeon's prophecy with a vengeance, this turning the sword in the Immaculate Heart of Mary—and for what? For the rabbis amongst whom He sat listening and asking questions? Hardly! He said it was because of "His Father's business." But to us, as to Mary and Joseph, "these words are beyond our understanding." Was it "His Father's business" to almost break His Mother's heart? Was it "His Father's business" to drive a two-edged sword into the soul of Joseph, who grieved not only for the Child who was lost but for the Mother who was seeking Him in such sorrow? Was it "His Father's business" to lengthen this agony through dark and dawn for three whole days? Before we follow our impulse and shout a passionate negative, let us recall what we have been learning about this Way.

Divine Providence, which is but another name for God, is bound to be more than puzzling; it is sure to be an insoluble mystery. We simply do not, we simply cannot, see the reason for many things. Why is this young couple denied children for whom they long, and for whom they could make lavish provision, while next door the mother already burdened with a large family, for whom the father is straining to make ends meet, gives birth to another healthy child? Why is it that this holy young woman brings forth a stillborn child, while a neighbor who has lost all faith becomes a mother to stocky twins? Why is it that this couple has a child who is a half-wit and that one a son who is a complete imbecile? Why? Why did that young man who was so full of character have to die while classmates who seemed so devoid of it live on? Why does this sick and crippled old man, who has outlived all who ever loved or cared for him, eke out his days in sheer misery while the strong, loving father of a young family is killed outright in an accident that leaves irresponsible ones unscathed?

The only answer to these questions and a thousand others like them is another question: Why was the Mother of God denied shelter at Bethlehem, given a sword at Jerusalem, made to fly into Egypt, and rendered childless for three endless days and three agonizing nights?

Theologians always say: God *allows* such evils. Caryll Houselander, I think, has improved on the word of these theologians when she says: "God has *hallowed* them." She calls such sufferings and soul-shaking sorrows "the courtesy of God" and says these but mark the "tenderness of His approach to the human heart." After all we have seen of Mary and from all we know of human psychology, can we question the accuracy of her analysis? Sorrow, we have seen, is but the flight of the Archangel Gabriel to announce the coming of Christ; it is but the wheat and wine which the priesthood of our baptism empowers us to consecrate and change into His Passion; it is the Holy Ghost overshadowing us that we might conceive and bring forth Christ.

We have seen all this from the first two steps on the Way. We have learned from our Mother that the most important word in the world is *Fiat*—God's will be done in us and by us. That one word, spoken by a sincere heart, is the alchemy sought by all the centuries and all the scientists. It turns everything into gold for God and man.

We have learned how to change exile into Eden. The secret is *Christ*. "Having Him we care for naught besides." We have seen Mary in Egypt and we saw her every horizon filled by her Son. Such is the way of a mother. And we are learning to "mother" Christ. When we have Him filling all our horizons, dawn and dark are but different manifestations of the same Beauty, storm and bright, calm blue are little more than left and right profiles of the same strong Magnificence. We are always happy because we have Him. But now comes a dolor in which He is lost....Horizons are wide and empty. The world has lost its light. What are we to say of this action of Christ? What are we to learn from this step by His Mother?

John Andrews has not dared draw the picture of this dolor. By some subtle artistic instinct he has been led to picture for us the joyful Mystery of the Finding and not that tumultuous sea of anguish which was the Loss. Yet the joy of the recovery suggests powerfully that anguish of the search.

THE PASSION OF MARY   In that one word "search" we have the very essence of the Passion that was Mary's. Her Golgotha was not outside the walls of the Holy City, it was in its tangle of narrow, twisting streets. His heart would be pierced by a lance after He was dead. But her heart was split wide open while she lived and knew that He was lost. Nails would bite into His hands and feet but never did they hurt as did the emptiness in Mary's hands and the unanswered echo of her feet as she searched, and searched, and searched.

Too often we think of the compassion of Mary as related only to Christ's own Passion, of her sorrow only as a result of His sorrow, of her suffering as related only to and as a result of His. But this dolor tells us something different, something deeper, something that reveals more clearly Mary's place in God's plan of Redemption and her relation to all mankind. Mary's compassion was related to Christ's Passion, but it was not merely the result of or her reaction to it. No, she had her own distinct agony and crucifixion of heart. Twenty years and more before He knew His desolation she experienced hers. In the words of Frank

Sheed, "It was part of the design of Redemption that while the Divine Person suffered the Passion that redeemed us, a human person should suffer a passion parallel with His." And for what purpose? To *co-redeem us!*

Pause before that truth. Look again at what John Andrews has drawn. The possessiveness of a mother is manifest in the way Mary clasps the Boy she has just found, but the awe, reverence, adoration, and love for God which were in her heart are also evident. One senses the very holiness of her love in the way she has placed her hand. And the position of her head tells us the story of the Passion she has just endured.

The picture before us and the mystery it portrays bares for us, as it will be bared only once again in all history, the terrifying reality which so many of our modern realists deny. Just as Calvary will one day hold a corpse of God which will be man's sin incarnate—so the Temple of God held this day a heart which for three days, though utterly sinless, knew what sin can do to a human being.

John Andrews was not only wise in drawing for us the finding rather than the loss; he was kind. For the sight of the loss of God in any life is terrifying, but what would it be if seen in the life of Christ's Mother? Sin is the loss of God. Sin is the corpse of Christ. Sin is Mary's heart during these three days and nights of her soul-wrenching search. Sin is a desert without oasis or even a mirage. Sin is death to man, the God-Man and the God-Man's Mother. Sin is the atom (frequently as small as that), which can disrupt the universe. It has done so already—heaven knew it in Lucifer; Eden, in Adam and Eve; sanctity, in Christ and His Mother; our world, in all us mortals. Yet there are those who will deny its existence! Small wonder our civilization is dying. Small wonder so much of it is already dead. How clearly St. Paul depicted man without Christ in his Epistle to the Romans. How basic to all his thought and all his theology is the awful reality, the world-cramming reality of sin. How terrifyingly real to any who think are the twin realities of Paul's life, and the life of any man who will use his memory and his mind: Sin and the One who is offended by it. Sin is as common as dirt, as universal as air. If Paul could use the verses of David a full one thousand years after David and yet have them depict the truth, what will these men who deny the existence of sin say when I use them almost two thousand years after Paul and have them depicting with accuracy the facts our newspapers give us without their factuality of sin? "There is," Paul writes, "not an innocent man among them, no, not one. There is nobody who reflects and searches for God; all alike are on the wrong course, all are wasted lives; not one of them acts honorably, no, not one. Their mouths are gaping tombs, they use their tongues to flatter. Under their lips the venom of asps is hidden. Their talk overflows with curses and calumny. They run hot-foot to shed blood; havoc and ruin follow in their path; the way of peace is unknown to them. They do not keep the fear of God before their eyes" (Rom. 3:10-18).[14]

That was Paul's picture of man without Christ. That was David's picture of man without God. That is a candid camera shot of modern man without grace, the sacraments, the Church. Sin is the one and only absolute dictator of the world; the strong tyrant who took hold of humanity with Adam's fall and will yield only to Christ. It is a fearful realization—this of the universality and the almost irresistible power of sin. But the more terrifying realization is that many moderns have lost all sense of sin!

The Communists are consistent. Their official ethics removes the idea of sin. If there is no God, there is, of course, no sin. But only the fool has said there is no God; and only a fool would say there is no sin. But fools can be dangerous persons. They can, they have, and they will bring death. That is why Atheistic Communism has been called "the most dangerous philosophy ever to appear on

---

[14] Knox translation.

the stage of the world." The world without God, man without Christ, are doomed to the tyranny of sin and can reap only the wages of sin—death.

Death is all that man can reap without Christ. Death is all that can be offered as ultimate by any who is not "in Christ." To deal death to Death was why Christ came—and to give us life. Mary, the sinless, tasted the fruit of sin when "the boy Jesus, unknown to His parents, continued His stay in Jerusalem." Mary died....

How many dead men people our world today—men who have lost Christ, men who are still in their sins?

There is a more dread death than that separation of the soul from the body which causes so much anguish all over the globe. It is that death of God within the soul, which we call sin. It is the extinguishing of the candle flame that was kindled at baptism and the leaving of the whole world of the soul in blackness. It is as St. Paul so graphically and truly put it: "crucifying anew the Son of God."

Do we really believe that? Do we believe that when we sin we are Pilate ordering the cross and the nails; we are Judas taking the thirty pieces of silver and kissing the Christ; we are Annas and Caiphas and the rest of the Sanhedrin urging the people on to cry "Away with this Man; give unto us Barabbas!" Do we really believe that when we sin we take hammer and use it on a nail that goes through the flesh of God? Or have we, too, lost our sense of sin?

The philosopher is often puzzled by this phenomenon, but never the theologian. The first knows that within each man is a conscience which has a voice. He knows that that voice speaks whenever man sins. He wonders how man can go on sinning after that voice has spoken. But the theologian knows both God and man a little better than the best philosopher, so he will tell you that the voice of conscience can be stifled by man; that man can so deafen himself that it is no longer a question of not heeding, but of not even hearing that voice. Then he will sadly go on to

GOD WILL NOT BE MOCKED

tell you that God is One who will not be mocked; that though He is all mercy, He is also a God of just anger; that He cannot allow His gifts to be spurned with utter impunity. He will tell you that conscience is one of God's greatest gifts—a gift of which God is very jealous; that if men will not use it aright, God will leave them to their folly and allow them to become stone deaf to the only voice that can save them from death that is death—the loss of Christ.

Paul to the Romans has been cited already. But how wonderfully apt are his words in this passage: "God's anger is being revealed from heaven; his anger against the impiety and wrong-doing of men...there is no excuse for them; although they had the knowledge of God, they did not honor him or give thanks to him as God; they became fantastic in their notions, and their senseless hearts grew benighted....That is why God *abandoned* their lustful hearts..." (Rom. 1:18-24).[15] And further on Paul says:... "as they scorned to keep God in their view, so God has abandoned them to a frame of mind worthy of all scorn...."

Then comes a passage that makes one wonder if we could not call this Paul's Epistle to the Russians as well as his Epistle to the Romans; a passage that brings us in at the end in a way that should send all of us searching for Jesus frantically.

The heathens had scorned God and Paul says God scorned them, abandoning them to a "frame of mind worthy of all scorn, that prompts them to disgraceful acts. They are versed in every kind of injustice, knavery, impurity, avarice, and ill will; spiteful, murderous, contentious, deceitful, depraved, backbiters, slanderers, God's enemies; insolent, haughty, vainglorious; inventive in wickedness, disobedient to their parents; without prudence, without honor, without love, without loyalty, without pity. Yet, with the just decree of God before their minds, they never grasped the truth that those who so live are deserving of

---

[15] Knox translation. Emphasis added.

death; not only those who commit such acts, but *those who countenance such a manner of living*" (Rom. 1:28-32).

The voice of conscience can become "like a bell clanging in an empty village," or like the Christ-Child lost and crying in a desert where not even echoes are aroused. And we can become living dead men, who continually kill God. That is the true picture of man habituated to sin: "without honor, without love, without loyalty, without pity—crucifying the Son of God anew."

Look at the hand of Mary pressing Christ to herself and realize that you will never live until, like her, you have "found the Christ."

This step in the Way is one which shakes us as neither of the first two did. To realize that the Mother of God was without God and that she was more stunned to learn that Christ was lost than she would have been if the earth had stopped revolving, all the stars had fallen, and the sun burned out—this is mystery! But we know that God revealed all mystery to us for our profit. We must plumb this one as far as we may, else prove niggardly to God and His Mother.

Sinlessness came to know the loneliness of sin. Why? Most say because she was to be the Refuge of Sinners and Mother of all the sinful. She had to know how we would feel after we had "crucified God anew." The answer has its force; but it is not complete. Mary had to know the awful loneliness of the sinner because she was and is the Mother of the *Whole* Christ. Now we are in Mystery that becomes ever more mysterious. Yet in its depths is the essence of our life and all our living. The darkness is well nigh impenetrable; yet it is imperative that we see. Let us grasp the hand of Paul. He will give us light.

Again we have to look at the text which we have seen so often already. The Douay Version renders it: "I fill up those things that are wanting of the suffering of Christ...." Msgr. Knox gives it this way: "I help to pay off the debt which the afflictions of Christ leave still to be paid, for the sake of his body, the Church" (Col. 1:24). Now the reason why not only the humble faithful draw back from such a text but even the learned theologians feel stunned by it, lies in the fact that we all know that Jesus Christ alone is Saviour and Jesus Christ alone has redeemed. We know that His passion and death were enough to save ten thousand times ten thousand worlds, each ten million times more sinful than our sin-sodden earth. We know He and He alone satisfied *superabundantly.* Yet Holy Scripture, which was written by the Holy Ghost, cannot err. Paul, under inspiration, could not deceive. And he says two things: first, that Christ left something unpaid; and second, that he, Paul, helps to pay it.

CLASP
THIS
TRUTH!

The truth contained here may seem difficult to grasp, but well may we say of it: "Clasp thou of truth its central core," and we add: "Hold fast that center's central sense." For it is all-important. Msgr. Knox would have it that we are under some sort of a *debt of honor* to repay the sufferings of Christ with sufferings of our own. The interpretation in the Kleist-Lilly translation would have it that Paul means here the sufferings we members must undergo in order to be *like* our Head. Frank Sheed, I think, improved on both of these when he distinguished carefully between the *Person* who suffered and the *nature* in which He suffered. The Second Person of the Blessed Trinity suffered in a human nature, which He had assumed. That, of course, is fundamental to the very notion of Redemption; for it was only because it was a Divine Person who suffered that the suffering was infinitely satisfactory—and only because He suffered in a human nature that humanity was redeemed. But Mr. Sheed does not stop there. He goes on to show that the human nature in Christ gave its utmost, but by a glorious provision by God the individual human natures human persons were to possess were not to be mere spectators in Redemption, but could contribute something of their own: "Human nature is privileged," he says, "to repeat in the persons of men what it has completed in the Person of Christ. Redeemed humanity can suffer in union with Christ, and in union with Christ these sufferings can become co-redemptive."[16]

Now it is the truth in that last line which makes life so thrilling even when to all human eyes it is as Shakespeare might say, "stale, flat and unprofitable." There is a co-redemptive activity to be placed by the Mystical Body of Christ, and in it, *every member* can play some part in so far as he places his sufferings, as Paul did, in Christ Jesus.

Well do we know we are playing with fire when we handle this truth. But it is a fire that can dispel the darkness of our day and of our individual lives, a fire like that Moses saw in the burning bush; one that warms and enlightens, but does not destroy or consume. Troubled by the fact that the Church teaches we have only one Saviour, the God-Man Jesus Christ, the Latin Fathers for the most part explain Paul's text by saying his words "the sufferings of Christ" do not refer to His Sacrifice on Calvary but to the labors, fatigues, sufferings He endured in His public life as He preached the Gospel. What the physical Christ did for a time, the mystical Christ must do for all time. It must labor and suffer to spread the Gospel to all men. Hence it is that Christ's members vicariously supply what Christ can no longer supply. That is why Paul can say "I fill up what is wanting."

But the Greek Fathers think that there is no necessity thus to dissociate us from the very Passion of Jesus Christ. They save His superabundant satisfactions by insisting, as all must, that Christ alone saves. But they explain Paul's part and our part in Redemption by saying "what is wanting" is the *application* of these infinite merits won by Christ. That application is made *through the sufferings of His members*.

How orthodox that teaching is can be seen by recalling

---

16 From *The Mary Book* (New York: Sheed and Ward, 1950), pp.239, 240.

a few lines from the pen of Pope Pius XII. In his encyclical on the Mystical Body he wrote: "Because Christ the Head holds such an eminent position, one must not think that He does not *require* the Body's help. What Paul said of the human organism is to be applied likewise to this Mystical Body: 'The Head cannot say to the feet: I have no need of you.' It is manifestly clear that the faithful need the help of the Divine Redeemer, for as He said: 'Without Me, you can do nothing,' and in the teaching of the Apostle, every advance of the Body toward perfection derives from Christ the Head. Yet, this, too, *must be held, marvelous though it appear: Christ requires His members...*"

The Pontiff then strives to clarify this mystery by combining, as it were, all that the Latin and Greek Fathers taught. He says: "Dying on the Cross He left to His Church the immense treasury of the Redemption; towards this she contributed nothing. But when these graces come to be distributed not only does He *share* this task of sanctification, but He wants it, in a way, to be *due to her action.* Deep mystery this, subject of inexhaustible meditation; that the *salvation* of many depends on the prayers and voluntary penances which the members of the Mystical Body of Christ offer for this intention."[17]

Now we ought to be able to understand better the action of Christ in *hallowing* this misunderstanding of His Mother, when she thought He was with Joseph as she set off from Jerusalem—and we ought to understand better Mary's awful anguish. If the members have to contribute to Redemption what must the Mother of both the Head and the members owe? She represented us, as St. Thomas and St. Bernard so eloquently teach, when she said *Fiat.* God waited the consent of the whole human race from the lips of the Virgin. He got it. But in that *Fiat* was consent also to the cross and the whole course of Redemption for the entire human race. She the Co-Redemptrix, represented us who would co-redeem. She had to know depths of

---

[17] *Mystici Corporis.* Emphasis added.

sorrow we cannot bear to fathom. And in Jerusalem she uttered for us what we so often repeat: " Why hast Thou done so to us?"

But the tragedy of our times is that this dolor is not repeated in its fullness by all of us. When we lose Jesus we do not set out in search immediately and refuse to think of anything else until he is found. The trouble is the same old trouble I have been pointing out from the beginning: *we forget.*

We forget that He is the Way, the Truth, and the Life. We forget that without Him we can do nothing. We forget that a branch cut off from the vine dies. We forget that we are His members. Is it not the most tragic loss of memory?

We are all more or less familiar with the words of St. Paul: *Mihi vivere Christus est,* which have been translated "For me to live is Christ." It is a correct translation, yet it does not contain the full force of Paul's words. The idea is: "For me, life is Christ" conversely: "For me, Christ is life!" Consequently, a man without Christ, no matter how energetic, vital, and vigorous he may appear, is actually dead! For he who has lost Christ has lost life.

SEEK AND FIND —LIFE

Now you can read more clearly all that is said by Mary's hand in this picture by John Andrews and all that is implied by that drooping head of hers. Now you can understand how kind Christ was both to His Mother and to all men by this seeming cruelty. He was giving His Mother the major part in the work of co-redeeming and giving all men a Mother who can understand what happens to their hearts, their souls, their very beings when they sin and lose Christ. Refuge of Sinners she is because she is Co-redemptrix from Sin.

Of course we will never know all that Mary suffered these three days and nights, just as we will never know all that Christ suffered those three hours on Calvary. But it might be well to mull over the statement made by many theologians that Mary was given foreknowledge of the

Passion. If that is true, then what a sword in her heart it must have been when she saw Joseph without the Child! Like lightning stabbing the black storm cloud came the thought: "Has Archelaus been craftier than his father, Herod? Tyrants never slumber. Had he seized Jesus and done to the Boy what his father had wanted to do to the Babe?" Like lightning, too, came the remembrance of the two thousand crosses and the two thousand crucified she had seen in Galilee just two years before. Was her Boy on such a cross now? Had she been wrong about the date of the Passion? That thought alone is enough to explain those words of complaint: "Son, why hast thou done so to us?" Yes, it was complaint. But let us remember that "complaint to God is adoration!" Jesus taught us that in the Garden and on Golgotha. His Mother teaches us the same now in the Temple.

It is right that we suffer in silence most of the time. But there comes a point when pain will cry out above our wills. There comes a point when it is right! It was right for Jesus on the cross. It was right for Mary in this dolor. It will be right for us when we are like Him saving the world or like her seeking the Christ. The answer most likely will be the same. It will be a question: "Did you not know that I must be about my Father's business?" Or as Msgr. Knox puts it: "Did you not know that I must needs be in the place which belongs to my Father."

Is it too violent an accommodation of those translations to say that if Christ has withdrawn Himself from you, as He did from His Mother, it will be for your sanctification—that is His "Father's business"—and that you are to seek Him within your soul—that is "the place which belongs to His Father."

I say that, because we can lose Christ and still be without sin. The "dark night of the soul" has become a quite familiar phrase, and I believe with good people it is even a more familiar experience. Christ does to them what He did to His Mother: He grants them a very special share in His Passion and in the salvation of the world. But it is an experience which does to them what these three days and nights did to Mary: it has them seeking, seeking, seeking.

So all of us experience the loss of the Child whether we be sinners or saints. If sinners, we can find Him in the Temple.

He will be waiting for us in the confessional and at the communion rail. If saints, we can find Him if we will seek as Mary did: totally forgetful of self, fully absorbed in the search, indefatigable until He is found.

That is the whole point in this dolor, this step in the Way—it ends in a Joyful Mystery!

When we look into ourselves with eyes that seek reality, we will find that we are very like El Greco's famous picture of Toledo. There is passion and power within; there is mystery and might; there is that bluish black sky gashed through with explosions of light; there is that upward surge and there is darkness. Kin fellow though we be of God, we know only too well that we are sprung from the sod. We were born in sin. Most have added to that sad inheritance by sins of their own. And there is no one of us who has not writhing within him like serpents the seven capital sins. But let us look even deeper and see the greater and the truer reality. Within each of us is an instinct that cannot only scotch those snakes, but kill them. Within each of us is a drive that can make us absolute masters of the flesh, conquerors of the devil, and victors over the world and all its worldliness. Within each of us is a hunger for God that will have us, if we are true to ourselves, doing all our life long what Mary did for three days and three nights. We will spend our lives seeking Christ—and finding Him!

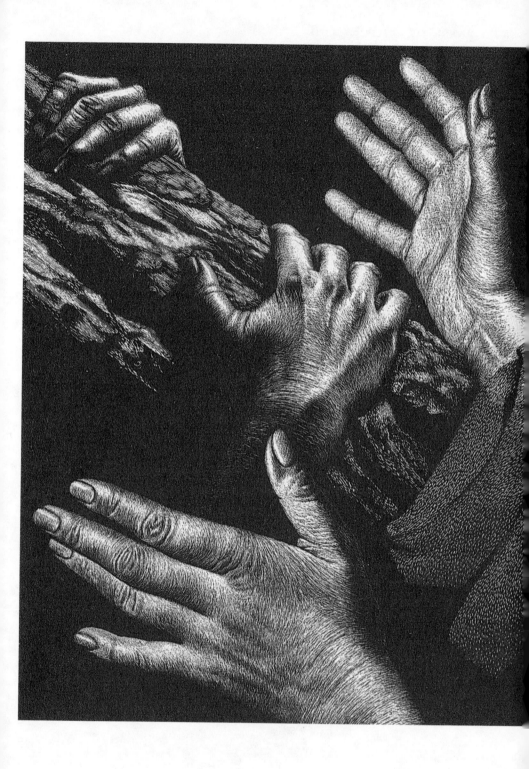

IV DOLOR

Mary Meets Jesus
on the Road to Calvary

HELP OF CHRISTIANS

THE cryptic answer of Jesus in the Temple leads us into eighteen years that are magnetic for anyone with an imagination and a love for the Holy Family. All the Gospels tell us is that "He was subject to them..." That is enough to give us meditation for a lifetime. He, the Son of God and very God Himself, was subject, was obedient, was docile and tractable to Joseph, the village carpenter and to Mary, the Maiden-Mother; God was a subject to those whom He had made. What a lesson for our proud, ever-assertive world! And in the next few lines what a lesson for us who are His members: "Jesus advanced in wisdom with the years, and in favor both with God and with men" (Lk. 2:52).[18] There is our goal on earth: to advance in favor both with God and with men; to advance with the years in wisdom! The Seat of Wisdom is leading us on, and brings us now to the sharpest challenge our manhood and womanhood will ever face—Mary goes out to meet Jesus as He treads His way to Calvary. The *Via Matris* is now converging on the *Via Dolorosa* of her Son.

For eighteen years there is utter silence about God Almighty and the woman He asked to give Him of her flesh and blood that He might have a human nature. It is a silence that has intrigued the best minds and biggest

---

[18] Knox translation.

hearts of the ages. What is the meaning of all this time given to obscurity? The world needed light and yet the Light of the World hid Himself in the tiny town of Nazareth, where He was looked upon as "the son of the carpenter." It is a mystery that fills cloisters and gives the benighted world other self-obliterating saviors. But it is a mystery that no one can think on rightly without seeing that it is love-filled. What a rapture for the Virgin who had to bring Him forth in a cave, lay Him in a manger, fly with Him to Egypt, to have Him all to herself in safety among her own people. Can anyone picture what life was like to Mary and Joseph? How little different it was from heaven!

Yet there was one stern difference. Mary possessed Him but it was only in time. And as time went on she well knew the day was drawing near when He would go away again—and it would be "His Father's business" that would take Him out of her home, and to a great extent, out of her life. The business would not be the work of a carpenter, though for its completion there would be need of hammer, nails, and wood. Mary had "pondered all these things in her heart," and dreaded the day when her Boy would go out to the world a Man.

The day came. He went. And after knowing eighteen years of intimacy and love, Mary faces three years which, in the gospel accounts, seldom show her to us, and when they do show her, we look in vain for that love, that warm and tender affection, which must have marked their every hour at Nazareth. It is a remarkable thing that whenever or wherever we meet Mary in the life of Christ as portrayed in the Gospels, there is absolutely no manifestation of that immeasurable love which must have filled His heart, no single trace of that tenderness we naturally expect from this tenderest of all men.

We have seen Him in the Temple give answer to a complaint that is all tears and all love with a question that reads almost like a rebuke: "What reason had you to search

for me?" That reply, coming from a Boy of twelve, to a
Mother who had just been through three days and three
nights of anguish, is more than surprising. And when we
know that Boy is God, the reply takes on the vesture of
revelation—and we pause long. Like Mary we keep the
memory of it in our hearts, even as those hearts ache for
Mary. The next time we meet these two in public is at a
wedding feast. The wine runs out, Mary turns to Jesus and
says: "They have no wine left." What was His reply before
the gay guests at the wedding feast? In the Greek it sounds
so harsh that every commentator exerts himself to explain
that we would have to hear the tone of voice and see the
light in the speaker's eyes before we could ever interpret it
aright. Jesus worked the miracle. But the reply still stands:
"Nay, woman, why dost thou trouble me with that? My
time has not yet come." We will hear that title (γυνή)
"Woman" once again. Granted that it did not hold any of
the offensive implications it can hold in our tongue today,
it still remains true that, here, Jesus did not call Mary
"Mother."

But the people called Mary by that name and in one
episode it leads to another manifestation of that remoteness, that bleakness which seems like harshness to those
who see only the surface. Jesus had been working miracles;
the blind, the lame, the halt, those possessed by the devil,
the palsied—all were cured. Crowds so hampered Him
that He could not even eat. Then cruel criticism and jealous opposition broke out. His own people called Him
"mad." The Scribes who had come down from Jerusalem
claim He is possessed by the devil. At this juncture Mary
comes forward. Archbishop Goodier would have it that
she came to save Him from His kinsfolk and the crowds.
At any rate she cannot get near Him. So word is brought
that "thy mother and thy brethren are without, looking for
thee." What does Jesus say and do?—The Kleist-Lilly
translation runs: "But he protested and said to the mes-

senger: 'Who is my mother? And who are my brothers?'
Then, with a wave of his hand toward his Disciples, he
said: 'Look! here are my mother and my brothers. Yes, anyone that does the will of my Father in heaven is brother, or
sister, or mother to me" (Mt. 12:48-50).

And St. Luke tells us that once a woman in the crowd
was so moved by the splendor of His teaching that she had
to cry out in praise of His mother saying: "Blessed is the
womb that bore thee, the breasts that nursed thee" (Lk.
11:27). It is a moving tribute both to Jesus and Mary. But
what does the Son say in reply? The Latin has a strong,
sharp negative: *Quinimmo*. Monsignor Knox softens it, no
doubt correctly, to: "Shall we not say, Blessed are those
who hear the word of God, and keep it?"

Of course we can explain each of these texts and each
of these incidents in a way that is highly favorable to Mary.
But the fact remains that she was always in the back-
ground during His public life, and when she did come
forward or was brought forward by others, Jesus manifested a remoteness that was very like coldness; at times
almost a rebuff.

The very best explanation we have already seen as we
studied the last step in the Way: Jesus was to have a
Passion. Mary was to have a Compassion. And we shall see
that all the more clearly as we now go on.

When the young Rabbi from Galilee was at the height
of His popularity; when people were saying: "No man ever
spoke like this"; when enthusiasts were proclaiming Him
the Messias; when they would take Him and make Him
King, we hear no mention of Mary. When palm branches
waved and a mighty escort sang "Hosanna!" we hear no
mention of Mary. But now that they have taken Him and
have made Him a thorn-crowned King; now that they are
leading Him out of the city over withered palm leaves;
now that He is a condemned criminal who has been
scourged and spit upon; now that He is the outcast of the

people, we see His Mother go out to meet Him!

John Andrews has given us two white arms stretched **TO HELP**
out toward two other arms that hold a cross. Mary's arms **GOD GO**
are stretched out as if they would embrace. The artist has **ON**
caught what the mystics tell us is true. Mary would
embrace the cross, not the Cross-bearer. Had she her way
there never would have been a Simon of Cyrene in the
story of our Redemption. The full import of her initial
Fiat is now upon her. As she sees her Son staggering
through the narrow crowded streets she knows, as never
before, how truly Simeon prophesied about the "rise and
fall of many." From out the eighteen years that have fled
since His finding in the Temple comes His question: "Did
you not know I must be about My Father's business?" She
has found her Son again and found Him in Jerusalem. He
is doing now what He had been doing then—tending to
His Father's business. As the Roman soldiers hurry Him
on and the Jewish rabble shout their taunts, she sees why
she had to hurry Him into Egypt. The Lamb had to be
saved for the Sacrifice. Her arms go out toward that strick-
en Lamb now with a love such as she did not have at
Bethlehem, Egypt, or Nazareth. Her arms go out not to
take the cross from Him, but to help Him carry it to the
summit where Redemption will be wrought.

More than once it has been said that it would seem
that God the Father loved His sons of men more than He
loved His own divine Son; for He allows the latter to go to
Calvary in place of and on behalf of the former. Of course
we know it is only seeming; but it does make us realize just
how much we are loved by God Almighty. So now with
Mary—as we see her stretch out those two lovely arms, we
say it would seem as if she loved us, His brethren, even
more than she loved her First-born; for she would help
Him, she would urge Him on to death that we might live.
That is why Mary went out to meet Him: to help Him on,
not to stop Him; to give Him courage and moral support

if He needed such; to compassionate in the truest sense of that word, which means to suffer with Him in order to save with Him. This picture with its two white arms tells us forcefully the tremendous truth that she is our Mother!

How are we to prove her children?

If Pius XI is right and we are facing a world that is at its worst since the Deluge; if the American hierarchy is correct in saying: "Christianity faces today its most serious crisis since the Church came out of the Catacombs"; if we have been right in insisting that the mysteries we have been contemplating are the mysteries of the present time, that each step in the Way of our Mother represents actualities of our own day, the answer to the above question is obvious. We will prove true children if we go out to meet the Christ who is under the cross!

Whittaker Chambers in his book *Witness* places his finger on the very focus of infection when he says: "The crisis exists in the Western World because actually we share the Communists' materialistic vision!" We have gone pagan. We have been taken in by the world. We bow before that "bitch-goddess"—Success. Yet we know not what success in life and successful living mean. In the words of Raoul Plus, S.J.: "Look how our Christians live. The greater number are sound pagans, among whom may be found certain traces of Christianity. Take a professed Christian and one who is not—a lawyer, a doctor, a merchant....How do they differ?" And the reply comes back too often: "How?"[18]

Must we not be as honest as Leon Bloy and cry: "What sorry Christians we are! We have received the Sacraments of Baptism and Confirmation—some of us even that of Holy Orders—yet, we lack *Character!*"[19] Yes—the character of Christ. How else explain the shambles that is our civilization where an Iron Curtain creeps and creeps and a Curtain of Bamboo ever expands, and God has to go underground? These steps on the Way show us as clearly as

---

[18] *Christ in Our Times* (Newman, 1953), p.65.

[19] *Pilgrim of the Absolute* (New York: Pantheon, 1947), p.224.

Holy Week shows us, how we Christians have failed both Christ and Christ's Mother. We have forgotten. We have forgotten that we are His members with a work to do! We have forgotten that the very first clause of our *Credo* is a declaration of war on the world, the flesh, and the devil. It is as Fr. Gillis has called it, "a world shaking manifesto, a challenge to Satan, an act of defiance of the forces of atheism, and at times and in certain places, as now over half the world, an enormous blasphemy against the omnipotent State. Since Michael the Archangel drew sword against the apostate angels, there has never been such a tremendous war-cry as: 'I believe in God.' All the conflict between heaven and hell is in those four words...."[20] Oh, if we only remembered from day to day that we are His members with a work to do, we would be afire with the same flame that burns in the breasts of the Communists, but for the opposite purpose. We would burn to "complete the Passion of Christ," to go out and meet Him with His cross, take it from Him and go to Golgotha, just as they burn with the determination to frustrate Calvary and enslave all men.

Mary's arms outstretched to the Christ with the cross tell us what we Christians should be. For they say that He has taken upon Himself the sins of the world that the world might be saved from sin's eternal consequences. They tell us that we, who sign ourselves with the Sign of the Cross, if we do not want to lie by our baptism and by every profession of Faith we have since made, should be ready to take upon ourselves the sins of mankind that mankind might know salvation. That is the Christian vocation. Christ Himself stated it explicitly: "If any man would come after Me, let him deny himself, take up his cross daily, and follow me." The work of His members is to die that men might live.

Now read what an ex-Communist says of his former Faith. "Communism says to man: Have you the moral

"A REASON TO LIVE— AND A REASON TO DIE"

---

[20] *So Near Is God: Essays on the Spiritual Life* (New York: Scribner's, 1953), p.29.

strength to take upon yourself the crimes of history, so that man, at last, may close his chronicle of age-old, senseless suffering, and replace it with purpose and plan?"[21]

There lies the strength of Communism. They have a Faith and a Vision. But it is faith in man. And their vision stops at earth's horizons and ends with life on earth. But they not only believe, they live their beliefs. Their vision gives them a "reason to live and a reason to die." The world outside Communism is dying because it lacks both faith and vision. May the present contemplation of the meeting between Christ and Mary as represented in John Andrews' drawing revive yours and mine!

We believe. From now on it is going to be with all our being, and not merely with mind and tongue. And the vision is that which led Jesus on His Way and brought Mary out to meet Him.

The impact of Protestantism in the sixteenth century aroused the Catholic world to a new enthusiasm for sanctity and martyrdom. The impact of Communism on our own century is doing the same thing. The Communists are actually sending sons and daughters of Mary out to meet Christ while He is under the cross.

But here in America Christ walks in great danger.

God, in His all-wise providence, has seen fit to allow two world wars to be fought away from our shores. We have never seen our cities reduced to rubble. We have never had to evacuate our children or watched while death rained down upon them from night skies. We have never walked through streets muddied red with human blood and strewn with shattered human bodies. We do not know what war is. We have not been awakened to its brutality and barbarism, its devastation—and the deep despair it breeds. Perhaps that is why we are not yet fully awake to what gives Communism its attractiveness and what makes it the deadly menace it is.

But God, in His goodness, has certainly given us warn-

---

[21] Whittaker Chambers, *Witness* (New York: Random House, 1952), p.11.

ing enough. Thirty years ago He gave us a full report on the Cieplak Trial when an Englishman by the name of McCullough wrote his book *The Bolshevik Persecution of Christianity.* To anyone with the slightest knowledge of the gospel account of the Passion and death of Christ, the parallel was most evident. Annas and Caiphas, Pilate and Herod, the Jews and the Romans had their modern counterparts. It was power and politics that condemned Him then. It is power and politics that are condemning Him now. It is in the name of Caesar that He is being sent to the cross from Moscow to Manchuria. History ever repeats itself.

But we Americans seem not to recognize either Christ or Antichrist. We seem like those onlookers who were in Jerusalem the day God died. If we will not do what John Andrews entices us to do with this drawing of his, let us pray that what Bishop Sheen fancied may yet be fact. In his *Life Is Worth Living,* he saw fit to say: "America is at the crossroads—the crossroads of the suffering world. It sees the world being crucified by Communism. The long arm of Providence is reaching out to America (as the strong arm of the Roman law had reached out to Simon of Cyrene) saying, 'Take up thy cross! Carry it!'"[22]

God has already tried to alert us in many ways. He is now sending us back our very own bishops, priests, and sisters from behind the Bamboo Curtain to tell us that His body bleeds and His Mother weeps as His members are scourged, spit upon, made to stand farcical trials, and are then condemned to death for having "been about His Father's business."

Will we awake before it is too late? We shall if we use our memories. The patient cures himself. We Americans are the only ones who can rid America of her awful forgetfulness of God. We Catholics are the ones who can best effect the cure by reminding ourselves always that we are His members with a definite work to do.

[22] New York: McGraw-Hill, 1953.

Has this crisis, which has the whole world cringing, ever been seen by you as a glorious opportunity? If not, the trouble is with your memory more than with your mind. You have forgotten what it means to be a Christian. Our religion is one of glowing optimism; for no matter what our state in life, no matter what the circumstances in which we find ourselves, no matter how seemingly insignificant or even despicable we may appear, we know that so long as we try to live up to our baptismal grants, the heavens can open any moment and a Voice be heard saying: "This is My beloved son in whom I am well pleased!" The stiffer the challenge and the more unequal the odds, the greater the opportunity for those who live mindful of the fact that they are His members with a work to do.

Let us awake to the fact that at this moment, when Christ walks in America under His heavy cross, we do not exist as baptized *people,* but as baptized *individuals*—a baptized baker, a baptized lawyer, a baptized politician, a baptized mother, a baptized stenographer, a baptized teacher, a baptized writer, a baptized nun, a baptized priest. Then we may realize that if the baker is to accept the challenge he will have to give Christ his whole mind, his whole heart and will, his whole being as a baker and show all that come near his bakery that a Christian is at work. The lawyer will have to do the same in his office and in the courtroom; the politician, in his specific role as representative of the people. It is the individual who is important; it is the person who counts with God—and with the world God made and redeemed.

How often we forget our own identity! We speak of "the country," "the State," "the government," "the Church," and "the world" as if we were not part of them! We need to realize that what Louis XIV said of himself, and which we take to have been so much arrogant, egotistical exaggeration, was literally true—and can be said by each of us with equal truth! The French King said: *L'Etat, c'est moi!*—*"I* am the State." And you—you are the United States as much as Washington, Lincoln, or Jefferson ever was; as much as the President is now! Yes, and even more specifically, you are the Church—for she is the Christ, and you are His member. So you are duty bound to wage "war for God, battle for civilization, fight to the last for ethical values and all that makes life beautiful and worthwhile." You are duty bound to go out and meet the Christ under His cross and stretch out arms as Mary did. But do not indulge in idle fancy. Your meeting with Christ may be as humiliating as Mary's was. He has few friends in the modern world; He has countless enemies. You may find yourself in your specific state in life surrounded as Mary was when she met Him on the way to Calvary. And He may look as bloody and as beaten; He may be as outcast and stigmatized by the highest powers in the land. But if you can look and see what Mary saw; if you will remember who you are; all will be well and you will "fight for God with all your soul, all your mind, all the love of your heart, here, there, and everywhere you go."

How do we help Christ carry His cross? How do we go out to meet Him as Mary did? How do we stretch out our arms? Christ Himself has told us again and again. The physical Christ could hardly have been more specific: "If you love me, keep my commandments." We know the ten that God wrote on stone for Moses. We know the six Christ has promulgated through His Church. The Mystical Christ has been even a bit more specific. He speaks about "the duties of our state in life" so often and so urgently that there is not one of us who cannot take his own spiritual temperature and count his own spiritual pulse. There is not one of us who cannot tell just how sound his heart is and how regularly all his spiritual organs are functioning. There is not one of us who cannot say with accuracy just how often, how far, and how willingly he has gone out to meet the condemned criminal whom we worship as the Son of God. All any of us has to do is ask: "How am I fulfilling the duties of my state in life?"

If each Catholic in these United States acted at all times as a Catholic should, the impact on Communism in these United States, and all over the world, would be very like the impact of the tiny stone David flung at Goliath. We may be numerically small in comparison with the whole; the "armor of Saul" most likely will not fit us; but we have the sling and we have the stones from the brook. Is it that we lack courage?

WHAT IT TAKES   It takes courage to be a Christian. It takes great courage to go out and meet Christ when He is on the road to Calvary, But just as a coward has no right to call himself a man, so a slacker in any slightest degree has no right to call himself a Christian. We cannot say that we are "of Christ," far less that we are "in Christ," if we flinch the fullness of crucifixion!

It is not easy to be a follower of Jesus. But it is a glory! And if Faith be the central problem of our day, then faith with fortitude is the only solution. Each of us who has been baptized is called upon to *be a witness* to Christ.

Do you know what that means? Whittaker Chambers, who will go down in history as "The Witness," gives as exact a definition as one could desire when he says: "A witness is a man whose life and faith are so completely one that when the challenge comes to step out and testify for his faith, he does so, disregarding all risks, accepting all consequences."

From those words you will learn what I mean by "a man," by an "integrated personality," by "one who possesses character." Chambers says life and faith must be *one.* That is, the individual must not only have a lively faith, but must *live his faith.* He must believe with his whole being what be professes to believe with his lips. He must say aloud his *Credo,* not with words, but with every action of his life. He must be a Catholic not only for the hour or so he spends in church on Sunday, but he must *be* Christ twenty-four hours a day, seven days a week, fifty-two weeks of the year.

Pope Pius XI, in *Quas Primas,* one of his earliest encyclicals, gave us as clear a description of what an integrated Christian is, as can be excogitated. By that letter he was establishing the Feast of Christ the King, and with the wisdom that has ever marked the dicta of the vicars of Christ, this little giant of the papacy came down to particulars, and taught that if Christ is to reign as King of nations, He must first reign totally as King of individuals.

Pius wrote: "Christ must reign in our *minds*—which must assent firmly and submissively to all revealed truth and to all Christ's teachings. He must reign in our *wills*—which should bow in obedience to God's laws and precepts. He must reign in our *hearts*—which, turning aside from all natural desires, should love God above all things and cling to Him alone. He must reign in our *bodies* and our *members,* which should serve as instruments of our soul's sanctification." There is an integrated man for you; there is the real Christian. One whose mind, will, heart, body and all its members are dominated by Jesus Christ totally and entirely, at all times and in all places.

That is no easy directive to follow. But I am proving that it takes courage to live up to our Baptism, and that we were baptized to be witnesses. What Christ said to Pilate at the most critical point in His life must be said by us every moment: "This is why I was born, and why I have come into the world, to bear witness to the truth" (Jn. 18:37).

Other Pilates may sneer and cynically ask: "What is truth?" But you and I must stand as did Incarnate Truth and give answer with our lives—and if need be, with our deaths. It is not easy to be a Christian; for it means you must be a witness; and witness is only another name for *martyr.*

Yes, to be a Christian means more, much more than most of us seem to realize. We forget what St. Paul said. We forget what St. Peter said. We forget what Jesus Himself has said.

We were reminded of it all by Pius XI in his monumental encyclical on Reparation, which is called *Miserentissimus Redemptor* from its opening words. There the Pope reminded us of our duty to be witnesses when he said: "The Apostle admonished us that by 'carrying about in our own body the dying state of Jesus' (II Cor. 4:10), and 'buried together with him by Baptism unto death' (Rom. 6:4) not only should we crucify our flesh with the vices and concupiscences' (Gal. 5:24) 'escaping the corruption of that concupiscence which is in the world' (2 Pet. 1:4), but also that 'the life of Jesus be manifest in our bodies' (II Cor. 4:10)."

"The life of Jesus should be manifest in your body"— What does that mean—that you are to have stigmata like Fr. Pio or Teresa Neumann; that you are to bear on your brow the wounds of the crown of thorns? Not at all! Not infrequently these external signs are the work of the devil. What God wants and what the world needs are stigmatized hearts, or as the Pope put it: minds, wills, hearts, bodies, and all their members dominated entirely by Christ. You can bear witness to Christ and Christianity, you can manifest the life of Jesus in your body, you can show all who come in contact with you that your heart wears stigmata by simply fulfilling the duties of your particular state in life.

It sounds simple. It really is simple. But it takes tremendous strength. In fact no man is strong enough to live up to those demands without divine aid. And there is the truth that brings out the glory of such a call. We need God. Without Him we can do nothing. But God also needs us. He needs us to bear witness to the fact that He exists; that God became man; that God died; that God rose again; that men can become like God. God needs us to be animated Gospels and give the world the almost unbelievable "Good News" that God is our Father and we are heirs to all that almighty God possesses.

Does the call frighten you? If so, think of the silent, silver steeple that rises above the Basilica here at **HOW TO DO IT** Gethsemani and dominates the monastery and all the lands around. How eloquent is that silent, cross-topped, bit of architecture to men who will reflect! What testimony it gives not only to man about God, but to God about men. As one sees it yearning toward the blue he is reminded of what God inspired His prophets to bring to the consciousness of His Chosen People time and time again. He is reminded of the duty incumbent on all creation to *adore.* He is reminded of the thunder of Sinai and that tremendous First Commandment: "I am the Lord, thy God; thou shalt not have strange gods before me." He is reminded of the Baptist, gaunt and glorious, pointing to one who walked by the Jordan and saying: "Behold the Lamb of God. Behold Him who taketh away the sins of the world." He is reminded of the Christ replying to the lawyer who had asked: "Rabbi, which is the great commandment in the law?" by saying: "Love the Lord your God with your whole heart, and with your whole soul, and with your whole mind. This is the great and the first commandment." He is reminded that one dark Friday there was a Crucifixion outside Jerusalem during which God called out to God for mercy on men. He is reminded of those challenging words of the Saviour: "If any man would be my follower, let him deny himself, take up his cross, and follow me." He is reminded that men can be more than men by the help of God.

For more than one hundred years Gethsemani has been kneeling like the Publican striking his breast and calling for mercy; has been echoing heaven's uninterrupted

Sanctus, Sanctus, Sanctus of praise and adoration; has been crying like Christ: "Father, forgive them; for they know not what they do"; has been turning to Jesus, when the rest of the world walked away, and saying: "Lord, to whom shall we go; Thou hast the words of eternal life"; and repeating Peter's grand profession: "Thou art the Christ, the Son of the living God." Gethsemani's steeple tells God that there are some men who believe with all their minds, hearts, wills, and all their beings that baptism makes us members of His Body who at the sixth hour, on the fourteenth day of the month Nisan, stretched out hands that had held wheat and wine the night before and allowed Roman soldiers to actualize the awe-filled words He had spoken in the Cenacle: "This is my body; this is my blood—which shall be shed for you." It tells God that there are some who understand what Christ meant when He said: "Do this in commemoration of Me." The Incarnation is prolonged; the Passion is being completed; God is being repaid; and mankind is being saved.

I have seen a thirty-third degree Mason, a man who was both Past Master and Past Grandmaster, a strong man with a pronouncedly virile character, weep as he watched a group of Gethsemani's monks file out to work. When I asked the reason for the tears, he answered: "I cannot help myself when I think of what those monks are doing for me."

What that silent, silver steeple and those silent, austere monks have said to God and man, each one of you can say by simply fulfilling the duties of your state in life.

We have forgotten that there is eloquence in the silent simplicity of doing one's ordinary duty. We have forgotten that there is power and terrific impact in example. A child of six was about to undergo a tonsillectomy. The surgeon, a fallen away Catholic, to ease all tension, playfully and paternally told the little girl that he was going to help her go to sleep for a while. Whereupon the child knelt on the operating table saying: "If I'm going to sleep, I must first say my night prayers." In all simplicity and with the full charm of innocent childhood she folded her hands and said what you and I have said again and again in our youth.

> Now I lay me down to sleep;
> To God I give my soul to keep.
> And if I die before I wake,
> To God I give my soul to take.

That night a fallen away surgeon came back to Christ.

We forget that silence speaks, that our mere presence gives testimony to truth—or evidence of our untruth!

Mary's two arms stretched out to Jesus and His cross. She did not speak. But her mere presence on the road to Calvary told Him He had one heart that was true, one soul that would go on with Him to the Redemption of mankind. Our mere presence in this world of the twentieth century speaks. Does it say all that Mary's presence said to God and man that fourteenth day of the month Nisan when Pilate gave Barabbas to the Jews and Jesus to the Roman soldiery?

It is not easy—but it is very, very simple!

You go out to meet Christ with His cross by the silence of your Catholic living. You give eloquent testimony to Truth by the simplicity of your strong Catholic example in fulfilling the duties of your state in life. Speech you need not make....

The gray walls of Gethsemani's cloister, the high walls that hedge in Carmelite and Poor Clare nuns, the grilles, iron grates, and thick curtains that hide from the world the faces of Passionist, Dominican, Good Shepherd, and Magdalen Sisters, and all those other women who adore God morning, noon, and night, speak with more eloquence than ever did Fenelon, Bourdaloue, Bossuet, or

Lacordaire. They not only say that there is a God who must be adored; not only that He so loved the world as to give His only-begotten Son for it; but very explicitly and with fine articulation they say that the Incarnation is being prolonged, the Passion of His only Son goes on, and that while Redemption is long over, the salvation of man is still being won.

And each Catholic father and mother who give their all to their children, laboring day in and day out to shelter these breaths of God from contamination by the world, focusing all their attention on the formation of their minds and hearts so that in afterlife purity will be prized before any pleasure, honesty above all gain, and sinlessness beyond all station in society; every engaged Catholic young man and woman who spend the time of courtship in deepening the realization of the sublimity and the sanctity of the state they plan to enter; the Catholic men and women who have given themselves to a profession or a career and accent the fact that they are Catholics first and professional or career people afterward, are speaking to the world with the same eloquence as those behind cloister, grate, curtain, and grille. There is a startling simplicity to our Catholic way of life. There is a power to our Catholic example which is irresistible. But we forget. We forget that the world watches. We forget that it hears our testimony though we speak not a word. We forget that we are witnesses at every moment and that the testimony we give will either convert man or condemn Christ!

In his moving encyclical on prayer and expiation to the Sacred Heart of Jesus in the present distress of the human race, known by most as *Caritate Christi Compulsi,* Pius XI gave as the object of our prayer what I have been giving as the object of our lives: "to preserve on earth *faith in One God, living and true.*

It will be accomplished only if we Catholics are converted!

That is the crying need of the moment. We Christians have to be converted to Christianity. We Catholics need to be converted to Catholicity. We followers of Christ need to know where He walked—and to what He leads. We children of Mary have to learn what it means to be mothered by such a woman, and what it means to be children to such a parent. Before there can be conversion there must be consciousness of our heresy; there must be confession of our guilt; there must be admission of our neglect of duty.

CATHOLICS MUST BE CONVERTED

Honesty is the prime requisite for a full *metanoia*, and anything less than a full *metanoia* will block our way to the necessary total conversion, that complete turning to Christ which alone constitutes the real Christian and the genuine Catholic. One must admit that he is sick before he seeks a cure. So we Catholics must confess our lack of Catholicity before we set about seeking conversion to the true Faith. Let the white arms of our Mother, stretched out to the battered, bloodblackened, tottering figure under His cross, serve as mirror to show us our real countenance. Let us stare at the reflection in that mirror until we know our own face. We Catholics are heretics. We Christians are pagans. We worshippers of the one true God burn incense at many a false shrine and bow before countless strange gods.

We claim to be followers of the poor Christ, the Man who had not whereon to lay His head—yet our idea of success in this world is a bank account and a thriving business. We look down upon the poverty-stricken as coldly as any Calvinist, Puritan, or Protestant who considers financial success as a stamp of divine approval on a sound faith, forgetting what God said about the difficulty the rich would have in entering heaven, forgetting that Christ said: "Blessed are the poor"; forgetting that He promised "Woe to you rich." How Christian are we Christians?

We claim to be followers of Him who said: "My kingdom is not of this world"; hence, that we are "Builders for Eternity."

Yet, who is more time-conscious? We have been told that "we have here no lasting city," yet we sink our foundations for homes that are intended to outlast the Pyramids and the Sphinx. We have been commanded to "seek the things that are above," to "store up treasure in heaven," yet the gnawing concern of our hearts—and our lives—is the security of stocks, and bonds. We quote the Sermon on the Mount, fashioning the Beatitudes into a happy litany—but to be applied to anyone and everyone save ourselves. Let those in the slums realize that it is "blessed to be poor"; let the handicapped and disabled realize that it is "blessed to suffer and be sorrowful"; let the underprivileged realize that it is "blessed to be meek and gentle"; let those who are persecuted politically, ostracized socially, crucified economically realize that "theirs is the Kingdom of Heaven." But for ourselves, we must be as wise as "the children of this generation who are wiser than the children of Light." How Catholic are we Catholics?

Do we even pray to clean up the slums? Do we so much as visit the sick, the imprisoned, the shut-ins by asking faith and fortitude from God for them? What is our attitude of mind toward dying thieves? murderers? harlots? outcasts? lonely children? helpless widows? destitute old age? Do you see why we need to be converted?

Let Mary's white arms serve as mirror, but be not like the man St. James tells about, "looking at his natural face in a mirror: for he looks at himself and goes away, and presently he forgets what kind of man he is" (Jas. 1:24, 25).

To be converted, we need a *metanoia*. To have a complete change of mind and heart we need to cure ourselves of our amnesia. To cure ourselves once and for all of this fatal forgetfulness, we need to be persuaded that by baptism we were constituted witnesses, and to be a witness one necessarily must be a martyr.

Note that I say we need to be persuaded. I do not say we need to be convinced. There is a tremendous difference between the two. The same difference we have seen between. "notional" assent and "real" assent. The same difference we have recognized between saying *Credo* with our lips, and saying it with our lives. The same difference between professing Christianity and radiating Christ. All of us are convinced. Not nearly enough of us have been persuaded. The man who is convinced accepts a truth with his mind. But the one who has been persuaded carries that truth into action. The convinced Christian and Catholic may have the devotional practice of making The Way of the Cross; that is, "saying the Stations." But the persuaded go out to meet the Christ on the way to Calvary and help Him carry the cross to the bloody summit The persuaded have had the *metanoia* which makes martyrs. They know that our Faith is not only a faultless philosophy but a force-filled Way of Life—the way we are on with our Mother and her Firstborn!

We all know what red martyrdom is. Not enough of us realize that there is another martyrdom which we call "white." But once we recognize that fact, we will see how true it is to say "every Christian is called to be a martyr."

In his latest encyclical, *Sacra Virginitas*, Pius XII dwelt on this truth and amassed evidence to show that it is traditional doctrine. He was writing about those in the priesthood and souls who have consecrated themselves to God by vows of chastity, but the truth of his words is applicable to all. He wrote: "How true is that saying of Chrysostom that 'the root and the flower of chastity is a crucified life.' For virginity, according to Ambrose, is a 'sacrificial offering' and the virgin is an oblation of modesty, a victim of chastity.' Indeed St. Methodius, Bishop of Olympus, compares virgins to martyrs. And St. Gregory the Great taught that perfect chastity substitutes for martyrdom when he wrote '...our peace has its martyrdom, because, though we bend not our necks to the sword, yet, with a spiritual weapon, we slay the fleshly desires of our hearts.'"

How often have you read and, perhaps, even spoken about "martyrs to duty"? That is the lesson we are to learn from the white arms of our Mother as she meets her Son on the road to Calvary. There is the martyrdom the vast majority of us must undergo. And let it be said in all truth that it is a far fiercer martyrdom than the speedy one of the Roman arena with its beasts, the speedier one of the firing squad, or even of the long drawn out torture of the Russian and Chinese Communists. With Paul most of us must say: "We die daily"; and some of us will live long, long lives.

It is not easy to be a Christian. But it is a glory! And the glorious part of our martyrdom is that we will be helped by the two white arms we see stretched out here to Jesus. There is the joy to be taken from this contemplation of Mary's dolor. The Queen of Martyrs underwent a martyrdom that was "white." She will mother us with every grace needed as we undergo our martyrdom. For most of us, I say, that will be "white"—made so by devotion to the duties of our state in life. But for some of us it may well be brutally red. Hence, we all need to remember this picture with its two white arms that help, and its two darker arms that showed us how to embrace a cross. We are His members—with *a work to do*. We are to witness to the truth of Him. We are to be martyrs for the Man-God. But we need not fear; for she is our Mother, who can give us the help we need.

Let us take to ourselves what Pius XII said in concluding the encyclical just mentioned. With that special warmth that has marked all His pronouncements he writes of his "compassion for priests, religious men and women who are bravely professing their Faith even to the extent of martyrdom. We pray God to sustain, strengthen and console them....May they realize that their pains are of great value in the sight of God for the restoration of His Kingdom in their own country and all over the world."

Do you realize that God the Father sees them and us through the red haze of the blood of His only-begotten Son? Do you realize that when He looks down on them and us there breaks on His ears the *Fiat* of Nazareth, the *Fiat* of Gethsemani, and Golgotha's thrilling *Consummatum est*?

Christ is on the way to Calvary. Mary, His Mother, has gone out to meet Him. Let us join them both that we may know the joy of carrying His cross and thus being a real Christian.

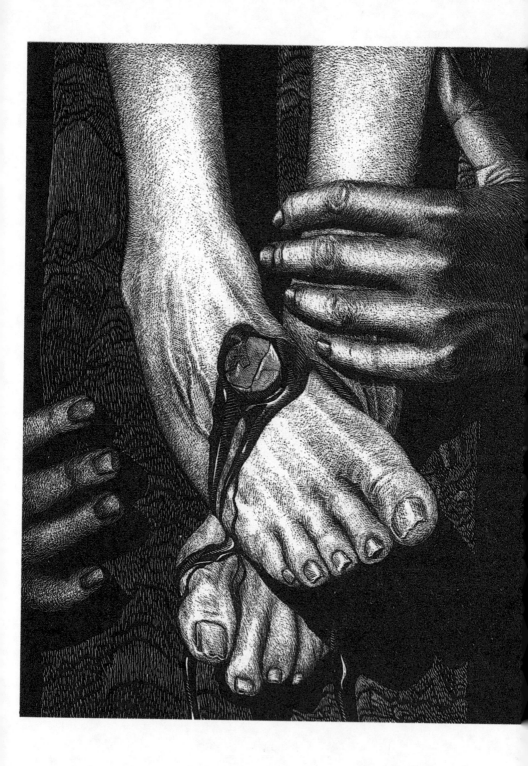

The Crucifixion

MOTHER OF GOD
—MOTHER OF MEN

"THERE stood by the cross of Jesus, his Mother" (Jn. 19:25). In these few words St. John has written the most poignant line in all literature. John Andrews, by crossing the feet of Christ and having blood well up around a buried spike, while Mary stands by, has given suggestion of an utterly unbelievable truth, yet one on whose whole-souled acceptance rests eternity for every human being in the world today. This picture says that God died—and His Mother was at His deathbed. Do you believe that?

Do you believe with all your soul that the sacrilege here commemorated wrought salvation? That this dread dolor the focal point of all her dolors—is the only source of our joy? That this death is the wellspring of all our life?

This dolor brings us to Calvary, at noon, on the fourteenth day of the month Nisan. It brings us to the midmost moment of the world—the hour to which everything from God's first *Fiat* of creation looked forward, and to which everything unto the final trumpet note telling Time's end will look back. It is a definite hour on a definite day; and yet it is eternal. Before Time was, before there was darkness or day, before the spirit of God had moved over any waters, before the first *Fiat* had evoked from emptiness an earth that was empty and void, this hour had been decreed. The Triune Wisdom and Power had made it the focal point of all Their Power and Wisdom. This is the high and holy moment when God's mercy and God's justice kiss—the black and brutal moment when God dies and His Mother stands by.

We are at that awful moment when sinlessness became sin that we sinners might be saved. We are in the presence of Adam and Eve and Satan, Sodom and Gomorrha, all the lusts, greeds, and hates that have scourged this earth of ours. We are in a sea of sin that rises in mighty swells and blacks out all horizons and heaven itself. Yet the focus of all our faculties: of our mind, intellect, memory, and will; the focus of all our senses: of sight, hearing, smell, taste, and touch; the focus of all our nerves, emotions, appetites, passions; the focus of all our beings is the sinless Son of the sinless Mother. The artist can only suggest. It is God, and God alone, who understands this dolor. It is God, and God alone, who can give us any light on its meaning and show us the very marrow of the mystery. We can but look as did the Israelites in the desert the morning they found the ground covered as with hoar frost, and with them say: *Manhu*—"What is this?"

And the answer that comes back is the one Moses made to the Chosen People: "This is the Bread which the Lord hath given you to eat." For the Lord had spoken through Moses saying: "In the evening you shall eat flesh, and in the morning you shall have your fill of bread: and you shall know that I am the Lord your God" (Ex. 16:12).

Does it seem strange that the bloody feet before us and the bowed head of His Mother should bring us back to Sodom and Gomorrha in one breath, then to the manna in the desert in the next? If so, you do not understand your Mass. Have you ever really assisted at Mass? That is what is depicted here. The parallel lines have met. We are on Calvary—and Calvary is the Mass. That is why we have to think of Paradise Lost and Paradise Regained; of Creation and Re-creation; of two Adams, two Eves, and the fruit of two trees. We have to face God's justice and yet feel the breath of His mercy on our faces. We have to think of the darkness of Egypt, the Paschal Lamb, and the Destroying Angel even as we watch the bright blood of the true Paschal Lamb mark the only doorpost that will ever save. The Mass is mystery; it is the summation and resolution of all the mysteries. It is the focal point of Mary's life; the focal point of Christ's life; the focal point of the life of every true Christian. Have you ever assisted at Mass? *It is the Crucifixion of God.*

How often we forget!

Like every mother of a priest, Mary gloried in making the vestments for her Son's first Mass. Jesus wore the "linens" she had woven for Him in her womb. His chasuble was red—she had given the pigment from her heart. Stole, maniple, and cincture were of identical color—from the identical source. Is it any wonder we find her standing by His cross? This is His first Mass. She must get His first blessing.

Now she understands the words He spoke at Cana. This is His hour. This is the hour for which she fled with Him into Egypt. It is the hour marked by Simeon when be spoke of the rise and fall of many in Israel. It is the hour for which He longed through three and thirty years; for it is the hour of His baptism by blood. Now she understands the words He spoke when she found Him in the Temple. This is His Father's business. It was for this she brought Him into the world: this hour of testimony and testament. He Himself had said: "For this was I born; for this came I into the world: that I might give testimony to the truth"— the truth of Sin! the truth of His love for all sinners! And only last night in the Cenacle He had told His intimates about this New and perpetual Testament.

"This is My Body." Yes, this thing spread on a cross.

"This is My Blood"—what you see streaming from head and hands and feet. This is the testimony and the testament. This is the Mass.

A SIGHT YOU HAVE NEVER SEEN   You will never understand this dolor until you have seen a crucifix. Oh, we have all looked at crosses and looked at crucifixes. But have we ever seen one?

The Apostles and Disciples, the early followers of Christ could not look so easily on what we view so often and with so little feeling or emotion. In the catacombs we find many symbols: bread, fish, the lamb—but the crucifix? Not so often. For they had seen the horror of many crucifixions of their own brethren in and about the city of Rome.

What we see is gold or ivory or fashionable bronze delicately shaped and holding up a graceful Christ in perfect symmetry and rhythmical proportions. We have grown used to the majesty and magnificence of arms outspread, head held high, and feet in shapeliness, His limbs in wonderful line. It is the Christ and it is His cross; but it is not His Crucifixion! Nor is it the Mass!

Well may we pause—all of us—at every Mass and ask as the Jews of old, *Manhu*—"What is this?" Well may we stare, as Chesterton advised, at every crucifix until it begins to look strange. Then we can answer our *Manhu*— "What is this?" by saying: "It is the Mass!"

You have never looked upon a crucifix and seen what the early Christians saw. They had seen men nailed!

> They'd seen them, twisting, sinking of their own
> Weight pulled upon the nails; with tongues extended,
> Heads that swung in torture side to side,
> That lifted up and cried for death in babbled
> Spurts of sound. They'd seen them. They had seen
> Men nailed...[23]

So must we look—until we see! For this is the Mass— the only important thing in all the world! This sacrilege

---

[23] *A Woman Wrapped in Silence* by John Lynch (New York: Macmillan, 1942), p.224.

which wrought salvation. We must look as Mary looked. We must stand as Mary stood.

This morning, before aurora and the dawn, I was on Calvary. I held in my hands the two feet John Andrews represents in this drawing. I held in my hands not only the bleeding feet, but the whole dripping torso, the hunched shoulders and the drooping head. And in a golden cup I had all the blood that welled up around the nails, poured from thorn-crowned head and was released by a lance from resting heart. I held it all! That which crimsoned the grass under olive trees, that which stained the white marble of Pilate's Praetorium, that which marked the Way of the Cross through Jerusalem's streets. Every drop of it was in my hands—even the water that rushed after the lance. It was the Mass. But how many thought of it as the crucifixion? All that was heard was "the white Heart-break of a Host," and some bells that made melody. But have you ever listened to what Mary heard as the first Mass bell? Listen!...

Calvary was dark. For three hours it grew dark and darker.

But His Mass went on. As candles, there was only a **A SOUND** thief on either side of Him—and one of those really went **YOU** out. As the sun refused to give her light, silence crept over **HAVE** the noisy hill. It was eerie, it was thick. It was a silence that **NEVER** quickened every ear for hearing. Mary listened. And **HEARD** then...

> ...A sound rang out to silence.
> Once, a single sound. Of iron beat
> To iron. There was a gasping in the crowd,
> And little cries caught rising in the breast,
> And ended. Then the mounting, breaking ring
> Of iron beat again to iron, beating,
> Beating, sounding to the air on strokes
> Of iron, beating to the skies that filled
> And rang and held above the world the iron
> Beating down and sounding until no more

Of earth, or life, or memory was left,
But only on the air, the beat of iron,
Iron, sounding, sounding beat of iron.[24]

That was the first Mass bell. Mary heard it—every iron beat of it. And "she was made alive in it." It loosed within her that maternal possessiveness which will know no barrier, that will strike aside all forms that stand between her and "her Own who was in that sound." She'd strain to Him!...

When next you assist at Mass hear at *Sanctus, Sanctus, Sanctus* the sound of "iron beat to iron," and know that it is heavy hammer smashing blunt nail through sacred nerve and flesh. Know that you are at the first Feast of Corpus Christi. Then, when the Host is held on high and a chalice lifted above a tonsured head, look up! Look up and see what Mary saw. See a naked Man squirming as He bleeds against a blackened sky; see a battered human body writhing on a tree, enprisoned there by savage spikes that have torn through sacred hands and feet; see thorn-tortured head tossing from side to side as anguished torso labors, lifts and strains; see the eyes of God roll toward heaven beseeching, as broken lips blurt out that soul-piercing cry: "My God. My God. Why hast Thou forsaken Me?"

Manhu—"What is this?"—This is the Mass. This is Crucifixion. This is what Mary saw at the Elevation of Christianity's first Mass. This is what you should see at the Elevation of every Mass.

"There stood by the cross of Jesus, his Mother."— Why? Because she knew—as only mothers can know—the deep need of her Son in this black hour. She knew that this was earth's first Feast of Corpus Christi; one that would demand everlasting reparation to the Heart that strained on the tree. She knew now why He had taken that body from her own very flesh and blood; it was for this awful

---

[24] *Ibid.*, p.222.

feast. So she stood by His cross to share His crime and, with Him, establish His claim. That crime was loving us too wildly, too well. That claim was to all our sins and to sovereignty over our sinful hearts. Mary knew—and on that darkened hill she was the only one who did know— exactly what was going on, She alone knew that this was the Mass. She alone knew that He was God of very God, and that this ashen face, streaked with spittle and with blood, was the very face of God. She knew that Jesus was hanging from those nails to make reparation to God the Father for all the sins of the world. She would stand there and make reparation for all the world to the Son.

Manhu—"What is this?"—This is reparation. This, standing by the cross of Christ when all the world has left Him, when every power in the land, civil, ecclesiastical, and social has sneered Him unto criminal condemnation and a gibbet of shame. And when the Man on the cross can look down now and see a face that understands, a face turned to Him as was His Mother's; then He finds what His Sacred Heart seeks—*reparation.* And surely, if there is one thing our sinful world owes our living, loving God, it is reparation.

This dolor was made anguish not by the nails, the thorns, the lance or the wood; not by that piercing cry: "I thirst" or that fiercer cry that shook earth and sundered the heavens: *Eli, Eli, lema sabacthani?;* this dolor was made anguish for her by what made the Passion agony for Him: our lack of appreciation, and the rendering void this utter emptying of Himself!

Nineteen hundred and more years after His cry of *Consummatum est!* had set the earth shaking, split rocks, and opened graves, we can hear a Mass bell without hearing the "sound of iron beat on iron" with the consequent tearing of flesh. We can look on a crucifix without seeing a crucified God. We can glance at consecrated wheat and consecrated wine without hearing Him ask—*Manhu*—

"What is this?" *Quae utilitas in Sanguine Meo?* "I am the vine but where are My branches? I spread Myself on the trellis of the cross that you might have life and have it more abundantly. I Myself am the living bread that has come down from heaven. If anyone eats of this bread he shall live forever. And what is this bread which I am to give? It is My flesh, given for the life of the world. But how many eat?" Think of it! We can call ourselves Christians, speak of Christianity and Christendom—without once saying Christ! We can claim to be children of Mary without realizing that Mary has only one Child—and He was crucified! We can say that we are His members without appreciating the fact that His personal, physical members carried the cross, bore the nails, knew the thorns, the lash and the lance. With right and fearful justice can Christ ask: "*Quae utilitas in Sanguine Meo*—What profit is there in my blood?" (Ps. 29:10)

This dolor searches the soul of everyone who would call himself or herself human. This mystery pounds at the heart of everyone who names self a Christian.

WHY?   Who is not baffled by it all? This dolor, which was the Mass, Christ's first Mass and Christianity's only Mass; this sacrilege of nails, thorns, wood, and lance was sacrifice of infinite worth—for the altar, the victim, the priest was Christ—and Christ is God. Here, then, was a death that could give life to a literally countless number of souls. Here sinlessness was crucified and sanctity that was infinite offered up. And yet our world, our tiny cinder of earth, becomes daily more sin-saturate. After two thousand years of hourly, aye, momentary, renewals of this Infinite Sacrifice, the redeemed race of man is still unregenerate. Why? Why is it that though heaven has heard in our mad century the "white Heart-break of a Host" three hundred thousand times a day, has seen the Son of God stripped naked, scourged, mocked and spit upon, has seen Him crowned and crucified, yet our so-called Christian era becomes ever more and more unmindful of Christ. Why is it?

You know now. This *Via Matris* has given you the answer in a single word: *amnesia.* Yes, we have forgotten! We Christians have forgotten that we are Christ. We Catholics have forgotten that we were born for only one purpose. We humans have forgotten what the lifework of each human is. We have all forgotten that we are "to fill up in our flesh those things that are wanting to His Passion, for His Body which is the Church." We have forgotten—if we ever really knew—the one thing that makes life livable and lovable, gives meaning to every moment, dignity to each least deed, infinite worth to what the material-minded would name worthless; we have forgotten that we came forth from the womb of baptism's waters with the same lifework to be performed as had the Christ when He came forth from the womb of Mary. He was born to say Mass. We were reborn for no other purpose. We make our lives a Mass—and His Mass our lives—or we never live!

Mary, our Mother, by leading us step after step, has brought us to the focal point of all human life and living. *"Manhu—*What is this?" It is to do as she did—stand under His cross, uniting self with Him, that the Father may have glory and mankind, grace. It is to make reparation to God and the Heart of His only Son. It is to make His Mass our lives and our lives a Mass. Mary has given us the only solution to the deep mystery of life. It lies in taking the ordinary things of our everyday life and placing them in the Ordinary of the Mass.

Have you ever thought what an *ordinary* life Mary lived? Is not her very presence here on Calvary ordinary? What mother would not do what she is doing? Yet, there is nothing in the world to equal it in worth! Nothing more that God asks or mankind needs! She made her life His Mass—and His Mass was her life! And we—we must take our ordinary joys and sorrows, our tiny triumphs and failures, our daily pleasures and disappointments—all the ordinary things that happen to us in the course of our day, and place them lovingly, confidently, generously in the Ordinary of the Mass. Today's headache, heartache, or backache is wheat for tomorrows paten; whatever success or joy, whatever thrill or consolation comes our way today, let it be wine for tomorrow's sacred chalice. And if humiliation or even disgrace should be our lot, that will be the drop of water that will be added to the wine and later changed into the very blood of God!

Manhu—"What is this?" It is making your life a Mass.

It is as simple as all that—and just as sublime as Mary beneath the cross or even as Jesus on it! Oh, how much we Christians have forgotten of Christianity—and of Christ!

Most of us are destined and predestined to be ordinary, as the world weighs worth. Yet we are the *pleroma Christi*. We "fill out Christ!" We are, as St. Augustine so boldly and truthfully said—we are *Christ!* So we *must* do as He did. The tremendousness of this truth staggers the mind. The prospect before us often shakes the heart and has the spirit quail. But that should not bother us. The same thing happened to Him in a place called Gethsemani. Even if we stumble on the Way that should not bother us. He fell more than once on the way to Calvary. But like Him, we must get up and go on; for, like Him, the world and God need us!

YOUR DIGNITY — AND DUTY How we have forgotten our dignity! How many of you lay-folk remember that you are priests? There are no quotation marks around that word; for I am speaking of objective reality and not using any figure of speech. Did not St. Peter, the first Pope, tell you that "You are a chosen race, *a royal priesthood,* a holy nation, a people that is God's possession, that you may proclaim the excellence of him who called you out of darkness into his marvelous light"? Did he not say just before that "you, as living stones, are built into a spiritual edifice, so as to be a *holy priesthood* to offer up spiritual sacrifices which will be acceptable to God through Jesus Christ" (I Pet. 2:5-9)?[25] Did not the last Pope, Pius XI, tell you that you, "an elect race, a royal priesthood, must concur in this oblation (of the Mass) almost in the same manner as the priest"? Had he not said just before that in his *Miserentissimus Redemptor* that "in the very august Eucharistic Sacrifice, the priests and the rest of the faithful must join their immolation in such a way that they offer themselves also as living hosts, holy and agreeable to God." Those words bare the heart of Christ's priesthood for you. The priest is not only priest, he is *victim* as well.

Never forget that you have been *ordained*. Once again I am speaking of objective reality and not using any figure of speech. For did not St. Jerome tell you that "Baptism is the ordination of the faithful"? Listen again to Pius XI: "...having become partakers in His eternal priesthood we should offer up gifts and sacrifices for sin. For not only are they partakers in the mysteries of this priesthood...who have been appointed by Jesus Christ the Highpriest as the ministers of such sacrifices...but also those Christians called, and rightly so, 'a chosen generation, a kingly priesthood,' who are to offer sacrifices for sin not only for themselves, but for all mankind, and this in much the same way as every priest."

The reality needs stressing. You share in the priesthood of the only Priest of the New Law—Jesus Christ. But that share in His priesthood imposes upon you the duty of sharing in His victimhood; for the only Priest of the New Law is the New Law's only Victim. Hence, when in the Cenacle, on the fourteenth day of the month Nisan, He said: "Do this in commemoration of Me," He was telling each baptized person that he or she must make the Mass life, and life a Mass, He was saying that we must take what we call our "crosses" and follow to where He made a cross a crucifix; that we must take what we call our "sacrifices"

---

[25] Kleist-Lilly translation. Emphasis added.

and blend them into His one great Sacrifice; that we must sweat in our own "Gethsemanis" and stumble up to our own "Golgothas" that "with Him, and through Him and in Him" we may save!

The night before He died He said "This is my body— This is my blood." Every day that we live, we are to hold out on the paten of our hands our hearts, and minds, and wills, our all, and say: "This is my body—this is my blood. Take them. And what You do with wheat and wine and these awe-filled words, do with me! Let the outward appearances remain; my face, figure, height, and breadth; but the inner substance, *Change!* Change it so that it will no longer be mine, but Thine. Change it so that I will always be what transubstantiated Wheat and Wine ever remain—Thee!"

That thought should not strike you as new. It is what John Andrews has represented in this drawing. Mary, at the foot of the cross, was offering her "Mass" just as Jesus, on the cross was offering His. It is the doctrine of St. Paul all over again. It is the very teaching of Christ Himself about taking up our cross.

But we forget!

How we need to be told again and again that Christ is expecting something from us; He is asking us to give Him what is still wanting in His Passion: to give Him the painful labor of our hands, the sufferings of our hearts; our tears, our flesh, our blood—our life!

Let us remember that if we do not join everything we do, everything we suffer, everything we are, to the Mass, there is very great danger that it all will be lost—and lost not only to us, but to Christ, and to all for whom He died! Our union with Jesus, who is God, is terrifyingly close. Arm to shoulder is not more closely joined than we to Christ. We are His members. We are His Mystical Body, and in that Mystical Body His Passion is continued and renewed. His Mass goes on—but only in so far as we unite ourselves with Him. It is the Mass that matters—and little else does!

What a need there is today for "little redeemers" who **GOD** will join their all with Him who has already redeemed, yet **NEEDS** needs us to complete the work of Redemption. **YOU—**

Twenty-two years ago, Pius XI, certainly one of the **TODAY** best informed men of the day, stated that "the greatest evil of the times" was not the economic depression that had given us the crash of the stock market, countless bank failures, wholesale unemployment and consequent world-wide misery, it was that deeper spiritual depression made manifest in organized, militant atheism. His Holiness minced no words as he told us how this new form of atheism had boldly proclaimed that "there will be neither peace nor welfare on earth until the last remnant of religion has been torn up, and religion's last living representative crushed out of existence."

Strong words. But for twenty-two years we have seen men striving with satanical ingenuity and energy to make good that God-defying proclamation—and they have known no little measure of success!

It was this same Pope who exclaimed: "Woe to mankind if God, spurned by His creatures, allows, in His justice, free course to this devastating flood, and uses it as a scourge to chastise the world." That we of today see that woe being fulfilled, that we feel the lash of God upon us, is man's fault, not God's. For in that same encyclical (*Miserentissimus Redemptor*) Pius XI told us that "the peoples of the world were called upon to make a definite choice: either to entrust themselves, humble and repentant, to God the Father of Mercies, or to abandon themselves to the mercy of God's enemy, the spirit of vengeance and destruction."

We know the choice mankind made. We also know the vengeance and destruction the enemy of God wrought. It is evident in bombed-out cities, but much more manifest in bombed-out souls. It caused Pius XII, in his very first encyclical, to write: "What age has been, for all its technical and purely civic programs, more tormented than ours by spiritual emptiness and deep-felt interior poverty? May we not apply to it the prophetic words of the Apocalypse: "...thou sayest, 'I am rich, and have grown wealthy and have need of nothing' and dost not know that thou art the wretched and miserable and poor and blind and naked one" (Apoc. 3:17). Then the Pope went on to speak of "the ever-increasing host of Christ's enemies," men who "deny or in practice neglect the vivifying truths and the values inherent in belief in God and in Christ"; men who "wantonly break the Tables of God's Commandments to substitute other tables and other standards stripped of the ethical content of the Revelation on Sinai, standards in which the Spirit of the Sermon on the Mount and of the Cross has no place."

But to realize the anxious need Christ has of other redeemers today, read Pius XII's climax: "Who could observe without profound grief the tragic harvest of desertions among those who in the days of calm and security were numbered among the followers of Christ, but who— Christians unfortunately more in name than in fact—in the hour that called for endurance, for effort, for suffering, for a stout heart in face of hidden or open persecution, fell *victims of cowardice,* weakness, uncertainty; who, terror-stricken before the *sacrifices* entailed by a profession of their Christian Faith, could not steel themselves to drink the bitter chalice awaiting those faithful to Christ."

The words "victim" and "sacrifices" in that passage are italicized to show you the kind of victim you must not be, and the kind of sacrifice God does not want. I have italicized them, also, that you might realize that you will be one kind of victim or the other; that you will offer one kind of sacrifice or the other; that your life will be a Mass—or a mess!

Today is a day of ultimates and of clear-cut choices. For the lines are sharply drawn. Either we stand with Mary beneath the cross, or we stand with the shouting rabble about the cross. We find ourselves either as members of the Mystical Body of Christ, or are found to be members of the mystical body of antichrist. We become totalitarian Christians and give our all to God, or we become totalitarian antichristians and have our all taken by the State. Pius XI stated absolutely that "in this conflict there is really question of the fundamental problem of the universe and of the most important decision proposed to man's free will: For *God* or against *God*. This once more is the alternative that shall decide the destinies of all mankind in politics, in finance, in morals, in the sciences and the arts, in the state, in civil and domestic society. In the East and in the West, this question confronts us everywhere...." Let me add that there is no middle ground, no island on which we can stand, no fence we may straddle. It is Christ or it is antichrist. Never were Christ's words more true: "He who is not with me is against me; and he who does not gather with me scatters" (Lk. 11:23). But this is the truth which makes our day a day of golden opportunity and one of real glory; for we can do exactly what Mary did in this dolor. We can side with Christ when He has no one else at His side.

In my own lifetime He could have sundered the heavens as He did when Saul was on the road to Damascus and asked the same question any hour of any day. Since the dawn of this twentieth century up to this hour He could have cried: "Why persecutest thou Me?" For in France, Russia, Portugal, Spain, Germany, Finland, Norway, and Switzerland, long before the rise of Bolshevism, Christ was persecuted in His members! Since World War I the persecution has been more bitter, more barbarous, more widespread. In our own half of the world, Ecuador, Guatemala, Honduras, and Mexico have treated Him as did the

HIS BODY BLEEDS

Roman soldiers in the Praetorium and on the Hill of Golgotha. Think how His blood has flowed in Russia, Spain, Mexico, and China these past few decades! Then you will understand me when I say "His Body bleeds and His Mother weeps."

But do not think that Christ has bled only across the ocean, or that Mary has wept in this continent only south of the Rio Grande. No, indeed. We need look at only one example to see how nearly Christ is killed here at home. We have shuddered over the two-edged sword unsheathed by Herod when Christ was hardly two years old. But think now of the more fearful slaughter of innocents done in our own day after almost two thousand years of Christianity. Statistics show that before World War II, annually, in our country there were as many as 700,000 abortions. During the War some sections saw an increase of from 20 to 40 per cent. Since the War we are faced with the hideous fact that over a million children are murdered in their mother's womb each year here in these United States of ours.

Christ died for each of those children and for their parents! Mary wept for each of them.

Yes, His Body bleeds here in America—and His Mother weeps. That gives you your greatest opportunity. You can help stanch that flow of blood and dry those tears by making your life a Mass and His Mass your very life. You will do that if you keep asking yourself: *Manhu*— "What is this!" and answering: "It is the Feast of Corpus Christi which demands reparation to the Sacred Heart; but reparation to the Sacred Heart is best made by offering up the Sacrifice of the Mass; and that is best done by always remembering that I am His member who must place all that I think, do, or say, all that I am, in Him who is the Mass!"

There is the joy of this heartbreaking dolor! It tells us that there is no such thing as a useless human being! That there is no such thing as an unimportant member of

Christ! Insignificant we may be; insignificant we are to economic and political society and to national and international society. But to God—and to our fellow man—we are Saviors, if we live in *Christ Jesus.*

Never in all time did man need God more. Never in all eternity did God have greater need for men—who would be His members and make their lives a Mass.

The duties of your state in life will furnish you the wheat, the wine, and the water! God will transubstantiate them if you live *in Christ Jesus.* Then there will be hope for the world that has left Christ as much alone as John Andrews has pictured Him here—just a bleeding body with a weeping woman beneath His cross. Sad? Infinitely so! Yet never did any human do as much to bring joy to all mankind as did the Human who bled and the Human who wept. And if we have to weep and bleed, we can bring joy not only to mankind but to the heart of Him who made all men.

It is the Mass that matters—nothing else does.

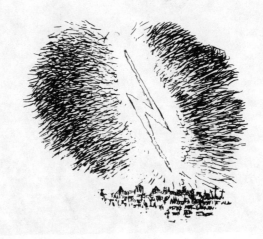

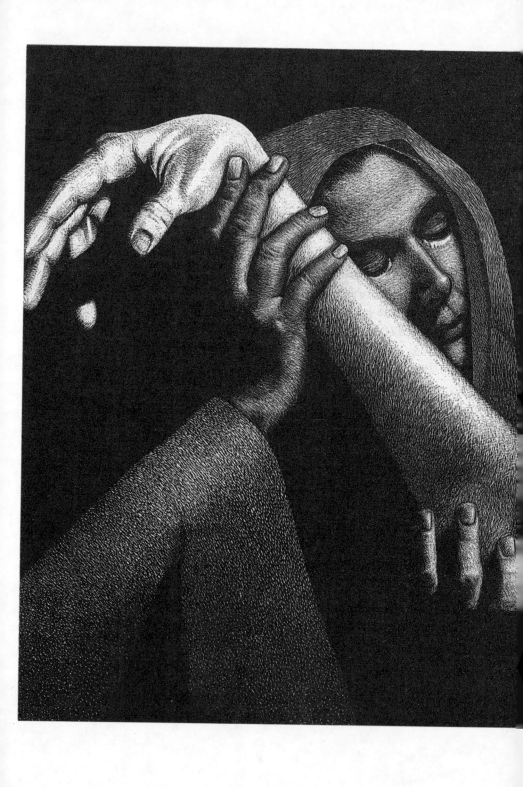

The Pieta

MATER NOSTRA

OF CHRIST St. John has written: "Having loved his own who were in the world, [He] loved them to the end" (Jn. 13:1).

We have just seen that end. It came at three o'clock Good Friday afternoon.

And every Good Friday afternoon at three o'clock there comes to our monastery a strange calm. Even those of us who literally stagger about the cloisters saying within ourselves: "Jesus, our Love, is crucified," feel this calm. It is not rest. It is not peace. It is not comfort, consolation, or joy. No. It is more nearly exhaustion. We have lived the liturgy; and from Palm Sunday's "Hosannas" to and through the Mass of the Presanctified we have been confronted with the *Magnalia Dei* in such a way that our whole souls—mind, memory, will, every emotion and our deepest passions—have been shaken, and shaken violently. We have not only been face to face with Christ, we have lived, as far as He will allow us and enable us, in Him. When He dies at three o'clock something in us dies. We are drained. We are spent. We are exhausted. We welcome the calm.

Anyone who has assisted at a long death agony knows of what I speak. And the closer the dying person was to the watcher, the more intimately does that one know the calm

I mention. So long as there is life in our loved ones we anguish and agonize with them; we sweat and strain; we work as if we would keep that life in them. Each heartbeat, each labored breath is ours—and we are tortured because we cannot give them our life, our energy. But once the soul has gone, we grow calm. We are spent. Our emotions are drained.

But there comes to us what we have not felt since the agony began—a calm. The finality of it all does something to our souls. We are sad. But there is a calm to it all. For it is ended—the watch, the life, the presence.

Not so with Mary. There are two more Stations to the Way of the Cross. There are two more dolors to her dolorous way. They, the Stations and the dolors, are the same; for as I said in the beginning: Parallel lines meet. Those of Jesus and His Mother are one.

The first Feast of Corpus Christi and the Sacred Heart drained Mary as Holy Thursday and Good Friday drain us monks. But a woman's heart, when it is the heart of a mother, is well-nigh fathomless. When that woman is the Mother of God what depths can we not expect?

Jesus died—but Mary's dolors went on.

She heard His last cry. She saw Him "give up the ghost." She looked up at sightless, staring eyes, the awful gray of the blood-streaked face, the open, loose mouth and that hollow blackness within it. She looked and saw that *He* was gone! He who had been her very life. He was gone! Her eyes were resting on a body drained of life; a body that was all her world; her world that was empty earth and nothingness. She knew now as she had never known before what it was to be alone. She had lost Him once; but then there was a search. Now she had no need to search. She could look on the body that she had given Him, but she could not find Him there. How alone she was! There was no time, no place, only He who hung so heavily from the nails. She looked and saw that He was dead! His head,

His features, His form—all were there before her on the
tree. But He—He was gone. The hill, the crowd, the
shouts, the darkness—all had vanished. One thing alone
filled her world, and that was He—Yet He was not there.
His hands were there, red, riven; His feet, too. His whole
lovable self—yet not a trace of Himself. Only the body,
only the body!

She knew—and of all on that Hill, she alone knew—
that Time had crossed a line; that these fresh moments
marked something different, marked something new; that
nothing would, or ever could, be the same again since He
had died. This was the hour Isaias had foretold and David
sung of in his Psalms. Now that it had passed, all that had
been foreshadowed or foretold from Eden on, had passed,
had been fulfilled. This cross divided everything. That
body sagging from those nails told how He had loved—
and how His love had emptied Him of life. For the fulfillment she was glad. She was glad, too, that with Him His
pain had died, that no more agony could be in hands or
feet, in lovely head—never again need He cry in thirst, nor
in that awful abandonment. Yet, even as this slight comfort came, a newer trouble affrighted her. This body, this
holy, sacred body...what was to become of it? Vaguely she
knew the law. The corpses of criminals won scanty con-
sideration from the courts. Some common grave, a ditch,
some careless pit or even the Valley of Gehenna might
serve for these three hanging here—the One who was dead
with the two who were dying!

Of all the hours of Mary's life, of all the dolors of her **THE**
dolorous way, this thought of sacrilege that might be done **LONGEST**
His body, this waiting while a man of wealth and a man of **HOUR**
worth went in boldly to Pilate, must have been the longest
hour she ever lived and the most bitter dolor she ever
knew.

Because St. Thomas has written truth when he called
the Eucharist *memoriam Passionis*, every true priest knows

something of the dread Mary knew as she waited word concerning His sacred body. How we fear any irreverence, any want of respect, any semblance of sacrilege toward the sacred Eucharist! And Mary was His Mother. And great indeed was the danger. She knew this helpless Thing hanging from nails was holy with the very holiness of God who had joined it to His divinity by means of His personality. She loved it as only mothers can love. She adored it as all lovers of God have come to adore it since this hour of waiting on Calvary. Imagine, if you can, what she felt as she saw the soldiers coming up the hill again, with lance and sword throwing off the rays of the late afternoon sun, which once again had come through the gloom.

Some idea of the quality of Mary's anxiety can be got from the experience of Fr. Robert Greene, the Maryknoll Missioner who wrote *Calvary in China.* During the days of his "house arrest" he had managed to say Mass and reserve the Blessed Sacrament. He told us he did so only after long prayer and reflection. He thought God had kept him in that part of China for a purpose—and that purpose in part was that Christ in the Eucharist might have one adorer. But suddenly, without the least warning he was taken off to "solitary confinement." And he confessed that what most likely saved him his mind during all the torture of "brain washing" was the thing that almost lost him his mind during the endless days and nights in "solitary confinement"—the thought of the Eucharist hidden up in his room—and the possibility, the high *probability,* of sacrilege when It was found.

In private conversation this "unmartyred martyr" told me how the ordeal was such that often after a whole night of "brain washing" he found himself staring at his fingers and trying to realize they belonged to his own hand, trying to count them and being unsuccessful, trying to say his rosary on them and becoming confused. But one prayer he never forgot to make. The *Hail Mary* might elude him; the

Our Father be as if unknown; but his heart, his whole being cried out in perfect sanity: "O Mary, take care of the Body of your Son!"

How Mary must have felt that prayer surge in her own soul as soldiers came up the hill and gathered round the crosses there. She saw them approach the thieves and with no hesitation strike cruel clubs across their legs. The sound was softer than "iron beating on iron"—but it was heart-piercing nonetheless. The more so as she knew they would next approach the body of all bodies! What could she do?

The Gospel tells us nothing. Yet John says he is to be believed because he saw what he wrote. Can we not believe he wrote what he saw? It is he who tells us that Mary *stood* by the cross. Would he not have told us if she cried out or swooned?

She had not cried out when that awful sound of "iron beating, beating, sounding to the air on strokes of iron" fell upon the world. She would strain to be near Him who was in the sound, but she did not cry out! And now when that other sacrilege—that mean and uncalled for crime, that lance-thrust which touched His heart and brought out blood and water finished all that sin could do, she did not waver.

We do not appreciate the uniqueness of our Mother! As she stands by the cross, a strong, straight, valiant woman who has just watched her Son die a criminal's death, then stood silent but understanding as a centurion sent his lance into His Sacred Heart, we can well weigh her worth and take measure of her almost measureless dignity. This quiet woman on this skull-shaped mound is the one and only human person in mankind's long, hard history who was conceived without sin—she is the Immaculate Conception! More, she is the woman whom God's great angel hailed as "full of grace'!' She is that one who sang *Magnificat,* prophesying that "all generations would call her blessed." She was right. She was all this, and she said all this because she was to be God's Mother. Of all mankind's myriad millions she was chosen by Him. And her response was magnificence itself. In a world black with rebellion she was the one burning light, the sole solid shaft of living, loving loyalty unto God. Of all the well-nigh countless descendants of Adam she is the one—and the only one—who was wholly His from the first moment of her existence, and will be wholly His everlastingly. Peerless she is. Peerless among human persons she will ever be. And God has given her to us to be our Mother!

And we—who are we?—We are the ones who murdered her Son. That is another fact we too often forget! It was just after we had spiked Him to His deathbed and just before He died that He made the bequest. That is why in the silence of our hearts we must ever supply for the silence of the Gospels and Tradition. The Gospels give us the name of the traitor who kissed His lips—Judas; the names of His principal accusers—Annas and Caiphas; the names of His judges—Pilate and Herod; the name of the one who pronounced final sentence—Pontius Pilate, the Roman Procurator. Tradition tells the name of him who drove the lance through His side and into His heart—Longinus. But who crucified Him? With Monsignor Hugh F. Blunt let us ask and answer—and find the guilty one:

> Who plaited the crown of thorns for His brow?
> Some Roman soldier, *nameless* now.
>
> Who hewed the Cross from the grim pine-tree?
> *Some* Jew—a carpenter—as was He.
>
> Who forged the nails He was fastened with?
> He knew no better—poor *nameless* smith.
>
> Nameless all!—for the sin and the shame
> Were done by one who bears *my name!* [26]

---

[26] "The Guilty One," from *Messenger of the Sacred Heart.*

While Mary still stands at the foot of the cross and Jesus hangs upon it, it is well to ponder long on those questions and answers above and realize that we—we are the guilty ones! We are the ones who nailed Him hands and feet, and set her standing 'neath the sacrilege. It is that shuddering realization that brings us to the heart of all mystery; for at the center of Calvary's teeming mysteries, as at the center of every mystery from the first *Fiat* of Creation, down through the *Fiat* of the Incarnation, and on into the *Fiat* of our Redemption lies the fact that God, who is *love,* endlessly pours Himself out in *love* upon us insignificant and infinitely insulting creatures.

That truth is staring us out of countenance as we look at this limp and lifeless hand and into the eyes of that Sorrowful Mother. For we were born on Calvary—we members of His Mystical Body. We came forth in these awe-filling birth pangs of Mary's compassion. Is that why she loves us so? Children of a difficult, dangerous and pain-filled parturition are not unusually the children of a predilection!

Before Joseph and Nicodemus lower the body from the cross, reflect on *the fact* that though our sins put Him there, His Mother *loves us!*

John Andrews has given us a new, deep, and moving Pieta. The right hand of God is to the lips of His Mother. Shining white but terrifyingly limp is that hand of Omnipotence. This is the hand that held bread last night in the Cenacle, the hand that passed the transubstantiated cup of wine; this is the hand that lifted Jairus' daughter when all that little one's world mourned her as dead; this is the hand that calmed wind and smoothed wave one night when hardy fishermen were afraid; this is the hand that opened eyes that had never seen, ears that had never heard, and set palsied feet dancing. This is the hand of God. Job says by this hand "all things were made"; Isaias told us this hand held all the waters in its hollow; and

David in his Psalms sang of how this right hand of God had held him up. This is the hand that was heavy on the Philistines, yet light upon Elias; strengthened Judith and was with Ezechiel. This is the hand that will not be shortened—though we have had it nailed! This is the right hand of Jesus near which, thanks to His merciful Mother, we hope to be found on that day when He shall say to all on His right: "Come, ye blessed of My Father...."

It is the hand of God the Creator, God the Avenger, God the just. It is the hand that in the Apocalypse opens the Book and holds the scales. And we have made it limp!

Mary is Mother of Helplessness again—and Mother of us who made Him thus helpless. St. Bernard has played all the stops as he contrasts the son she received and the Son she lost as she stood 'neath the cross. It is masterly writing and moving antithesis. There is no one who cannot follow his thought and agree with his balance of facts. Yet, now that we are conscious of the doctrine so long dormant, the truth of the Mystical Body of Christ, we can understand what Bernard's superb prose would never enable us to understand. Mary loves us the men and women who put Jesus on the cross. How can that be if, as Bernard points out, there was an exchange made while Christ hung on that cross. He says: "For Jesus, she was given John; for the Lord, the servant; for the Master, the disciple; for the Son of God, the son of Zebedee; for the true God, a mere man." We add that in John she was given each of us, and through John each of us received her. And who of us can feel as worthy as John was? Yet she received us—and she loves us!

Somewhere, Charles Journet, writing of this exchange said: "For John the words of Christ—Behold thy mother—were a joy unspeakable. But to Mary they were shattering." Then he quickly adds: "Of course she loved the disciple Jesus loved. But what an exchange!"

Bernard and Journet are right. They tell us truth. Yet

there is a deeper depth to the truth which neither of them touch. It lies in the fact that *we are His members!* If a Bavarian peasant woman could say with utter conviction: "There is only one child in all the world: He is Jesus," what could Mary Immaculate think and say?

There was an exchange! Jesus was to live on earth but no longer in the physical body He had taken from Mary's womb; He would live in the mystical body He would assume from the womb of mankind. And Mary, physical mother of the first, would be spiritual mother of the second. That is why she loves us so! We, as St. Augustine said, are Jesus. We, therefore, are Mary's children. What a challenge lies in that truth!

Any picture of the Virgin and her Son, be it that of **IT IS NOT** Christmas or Calvary, the Madonna or the Pieta, should **EASY** pose questions to each of us about our character and manner of life. Are we living as children of such a Mother and does our character stand out as similar to that of such a Brother? Let us face the fact that it is not easy to be a child of Mary. We may have to hang on nails—and be let down as limp as is this right hand which Mary lifts to her cheek!

That has already happened in America—both to the north of us and to the south. Isaac Jogues and Jean de Brebeuf with their six companions tell us it is not easy to be a child of Mary. Fr. Miguel Pro, S.J., and the numberless priests who suffered martyrdom in Mexico tell us it is not easy to be a child of Mary. The nuns, the priests, the prelates who come back to us from China after knowing "house arrest," "solitary confinement," and then "brain washing" tell us it is not easy to be a child of Mary. Now, when it would seem that the very powers of hell have been given extra liberty, we all know it is not easy to be a child of Mary.

Women and girls know it is not easy to be daring enough not to be "daring" in their dress; it is not easy to defy the very defiant styles, and be as modest as was Mary.

Men and young men in politics or business, in the professions or the trades know it is not easy to be honest, to uphold principle in the face of compromise and mere policy, to be completely straight when so many are crooked and being called clever for their crookedness. Mothers and fathers, husbands and wives, children of maturity and youngsters still in their teens can tell us that it is not easy to be what we ought to be after Christ has taken us to Himself while hanging on the cross.

Yes, that is the deeper truth of that "exchange." Jesus, rather than giving His Mother away, took other brothers and sisters to Himself, made mortals members of His sacred body, and thus made life for all humans a romance of living up to the nobility He has conferred on them. It is no easy thing to do. But it is a romance to attempt—and a glory to achieve. To be a child of Mary is not easy. But there is nothing in the world half so glorious!

It makes little difference whether you focus on the limp white hand or the hooded sorrowful face in this drawing of the sixth dolor. The lesson is the same. The hand tells you how to end; the hooded face, how to go on. To be a child of Mary means that you must be able to say as Jesus said: "I do always the things that please Him....My meat is to do the will of Him who sent me....In the head of the book it is written: behold I come to do thy will, O God." To be a child of Mary means that you must ever be ready to say what she said to Gabriel: "Behold the handmaid of the Lord—Be it done unto me according to thy word—thy will—O God." To be a child of Mary means that we must be able to sum up our lives and the work of our lives as Jesus did when darkness was over all the world and He had but a few more breaths to draw. It means that we can die saying: "It is consummated—I have completed the work You gave me to do, O God. Into Thy hands I commend my spirit."

Do you know what the will of God is in your regard? **WHAT**
St. Paul has told you, and in telling you, has given such **GOD**
clear delineation to what it means to be a child of Mary **WANTS**
that we can say that he has etched it as with acid on bronze **OF YOU**
that will ever endure. Paul said: "This is the will of God—
your sanctification." To be a child of Mary means to be a
saint. That is your destiny. That is your duty. That is the
one work of your life and your life's only work. Failing
that, no matter what else you may achieve, you have failed
dismally.

Leon Bloy's last line in his novel *The Woman Who Was
Poor* has been quoted again and again. For everyone knows
that it is truth as true as God. He has his heroine say:
"There is only one sorrow: not to be a saint." Do you see,
then, how happy God wants you to be? He has willed that
you be a saint; has made it the whole purpose of your life
and the only meaning of all your living. And while He has
not made the attainment of this one goal the easiest thing
in the world, He most certainly has put zest into our exile
and made life on earth a blood-stirring challenge. Further,
He has made this cloudkissing peak not only possible of
scaling, but, to all who will be mindful of their own nobility, highly probable of reaching. Life is a divine adventure;
for God alone is holy, God alone is substantial sanctity. So
whatever holiness or sanctity humans know, it comes from
God; it is a share in His nature! There is the goal of life—
sharing the Godhead—living with the very life of God—
being somehow or other one with the Trinity! It was for
this that Jesus Christ prayed the last night He was on
earth: That we may be one as He and the Father are one.

Who can find any boredom in life, experience ennui
while living, know anything but thrill and romance,
adventure and zest, so long as he or she is mindful of the
goal God has set us?

But we forget! We forget!

How many of us have ever resolved with a real resolve

to be a saint? We shrink back smiling shyly. We even deem it virtuous; calling it humility or avoidance of presumption. It is neither! It most likely is human respect, which is only a form of pride, and cowardice—or it is unadulterated sloth. It costs to live up to our dignity. It costs to be a saint. But woe to that man or woman who will not pay the price! Let us never again forget, that only saints get into heaven! If we really intend to get to heaven, it is high time for each of us to resolve to be a saint.

In other words, if we want to die as Jesus did, and be received into Mary's arms, we have to live as Jesus did. He was the Saint of saints. He showed us the way to sainthood by "doing always the things that please him—God, the Father." That simply means always doing God's will.

Conceive clearly just in what sanctity consists, else you will never attain the only object of existence. It does not consist in the extraordinary! Not in visions, rapts, ecstasies, interior locutions, the gifts of miracles, prophecy, or tears! It is not necessary that we receive the stigmata on our hands, feet, and side. We need not be graced with the ability to read hearts or be in more than one place at one time. But it does demand that we be in the one place the duty of our state in life requires that we be, and that we be doing our specific duty with the intention of fulfilling God's will.

We have coursed through the life of the most saintly human person ever to live. How many miracles have we seen her perform? Apart from the Annunciation, how many visions did Mary have? When she sang her beautiful *Magnificat* she was aglow with love and gratitude, but she was not in what we have come to term an ecstasy. Our Mother shows us the way to sanctity. It lies in the ordinary; it consists in the usual; it is made up of what some call the humdrum round of daily duties. But all must be elevated above the ordinary! They must be placed, as we have said, in the Ordinary of the Mass; they must be

placed in *Christ Jesus*. Then they will win for us the one
success in life. And, thanks be to God and His infinite
generosity, they will win salvation for more than ourselves.

As we look at the dead body of the ever living God in **YOU HAVE**
the arms of His sorrowful Mother, it behooves us to **NOT BEEN**
remember that while the whole human race was *redeemed* **SAVED**
by this Passion and Death, not a single soul was *saved* by
this Infinite Sacrifice.

That insistence on the difference between Redemption
and Salvation always shocks. The Passion and the
Compassion represented in these drawings were enough to
redeem ten thousand worlds. The Person who suffered on
that cross was the Second Person of the Trinity. He was
God. Therefore, His Sacrifice was of *infinite* value. She
who shared it all with Him was the one and only sinless
human person in all creation, the greatest of all the saints,
the very Queen of Heaven and earth. With such sanctity
dedicated to a Sacrifice whose only purpose was
Redemption many want to know how it is that we can
speak of Christ suffering today; of humans filling up what
is wanting to this Infinite Sacrifice, this superabundant
Redemption; of mankind co-operating in this work of
God and helping to save fellow human beings.

There are grounds for such objections. St. Paul has
told us again and again that "Christ dies no more." We
know that His glorified body knows no lash, nails, or
lance. We want to know how anything can be "wanting"
to what is already infinite; how what is superabundant can
yet be "filled up." Finally, we call Christ not only
Redeemer, but Saviour. What then is this talk of humans
being Christ's coadjutors in salvation?

As Mary washes His body and thinks back on those
blessed infant days when she washed and dressed Him
again and again; as she tries to untangle the blood-clotted
hair she had so often combed and curled in Bethlehem
and Egypt; as she kisses gaping wounds and thinks back

on the days she used to kiss away His pain whenever He fell while playing in Nazareth; as she sees the dark coming on and thinks back on those other darknesses when she sang Him to sleep; as she closes eyes that had so often smiled into hers, and mouth that had so often kissed her cheek; as she folds nail-riven hands and wraps the dead body in a funeral shroud just as she had once wrapped it in swaddling clothes, let us face and answer the objections we have raised, so that life will hold no further questions and pain never again present us with a problem.

How can Christ, who lives now in a body that is glorified, suffer?—In the same manner that the eternally impassible God underwent a Passion the like of which earth had never before seen, nor will ever look upon again. Namely, *by assuming a body!* God, as God, could not suffer. He had to ask a little Maid in Nazareth if she would give Him flesh and blood, a human body, so that He might redeem mankind by suffering in it.

Grasp that truth firmly. Philosophy tells that: *Actiones et passiones sunt suppositorum,* which means that it is the *person* who acts or suffers, not the body or its organs. Anyone who has had a toothache knows that. It is not the tooth that aches; but *we* who ache *in* the tooth. When we stub our toe or bark our shins, it is not the toe or the shin that hurts, but *we* who feel the hurt in the toe or shin. It is the *person* who suffers and suffers in his members! Don't you see then, that just as Jesus agonized in the body He took from the womb of His immaculate Mother two thousand years ago, and thus redeemed the world, so now the same Christ suffers in the body He has taken from the womb of mankind, and thus saves the human individual? Actions belong to the Person who has the body. Sufferings belong to the One who feels those sufferings in his bodily members.

Perhaps this will clarify and fix the truth in your mind: This morning, I and every priest of God who offered

Mass, held a chalice containing wine before our breasts
and prayed almighty God to accept it *pro nostra et totius
mundi salute*—for the *salvation* of the entire world. But
when we bent over that same chalice to consecrate that
same wine and change it into the very blood that crimsoned Calvary's cross and which Mary found coagulated
and black on His face and hands and whole torso, our
prayer changed. We said: *qui pro vobis et pro multis effun-
detur.* We did not say "for *all*"; we said "for *many*." Why
this startling difference?—Because there is a startling difference between Redemption and Salvation.

There is not a single human being in this world—
there never was and there never will be—who has not
already been *redeemed*. But there is not a single human
being on earth today who has already been *saved!* The difference is truly frightening. The fright comes from the fact
that we who have already been redeemed, can yet be
damned. Though Jesus opened for us the gates of heaven
with hands that had been nail-pierced, we can yet go down
into hell.

This dolor of Mary's can be a dolor for us if we do not
grasp the difference between redemption and salvation.
Redemption is an accomplished fact; salvation for us is
still only a possibility. Redemption has already been fully
achieved by Jesus Christ for all mankind; but the salvation
of the individual humans now living on earth is yet to be
achieved by Christ in us, and by us in Christ Jesus. That is
why it is so important to remember that we are His members, and never to forget we have one work to do! In His
physical body, by this awful Passion and Death, Jesus
Christ *redeemed.* But it is only in His mystical body and
through its "passion" that He can *save.* Redemption was
His work—and His work alone. Mother Mary compas-
sionated and, by associating it all with His Passion, merited the title of Co-Redemptrix. But strictly speaking Christ
alone redeemed. That work is over and done with; it was

perfectly achieved; it is wholly completed, infinite in its worth, superabundant in its merit. But salvation is a matter of co-operation. Jesus does not do it alone!

Now we can complete that famous dictum of St. Augustine and make it theologically exact, by saying, "God made you without yourself; God redeemed you without yourself; but God will not save you without yourself!"

There is deep pathos in the way the Council of Trent has expressed this truth. It has said: "Though Christ died for all; yet, not all will receive the benefit of His Death!" That is an echo of the line in the Psalm we have already quoted: "*Quae utilitas in Sanguine Meo?*—What profit is there in my blood?" That is the stark reality that faces all who think as they look at this limp white hand and the immaculate Mother sorrowing over it. This infinite sacrifice will have been in vain for many simply because not all of us will resolve, and live the resolve, to be saints!

As I write I know that out of the almost two billion persons on the earth at this moment, not more than one third of them knows so much as the name of the One who died that they might live eternally. And as one very observant mystic remarked: "Out of that third, close to ninety-nine per cent of them know it in vain." Is that not enough to set the nine choirs of the angels weeping?

A GLORIOUS TIME TO BE ALIVE But we of this mad mid-twentieth century can rejoice that there are those who gladly give their all that He shall not have bled in vain, nor she have wept without garnering souls by her sorrows. We can rejoice that we live in the greatest age of martyrs and martyrdom that the Church has ever known. We can bless God that He allows us to live at a time when His Son's Mystical body is suffering as never before and thus bringing the fruits of the suffering of His physical body clear across the globe, applying them to countless souls who would never have lived the life of all living had not these men and women borne witness to

Christ by giving up their lives.

It is no wonder that Mary loves our day and age. Thanks to persecution, we are giving more to her Son than any other age or day since Calvary. The Nazis in Germany, Austria, and Poland; the Reds in all the Balkan lands, Russia, and now in China, have done more for heaven than ever did the Roman Caesars, the kings and queens of England, or the madmen of the French Revolution. They have done more for earth, too. For while peopling heaven with martyrs, they have also spread far and wide the grace of Christ Jesus, thanks to the oneness of His mystical body.

It is true that God looks down on what is often worse than Sodom and Gomorrha; listens to what is worse than Babel or Babylon; sees what deserves more than a Deluge. Yet at the same time children of Mary, members of Christ, are setting heaven and its high halls ringing with that irresistible cry: "Father, forgive them; for they know not what they do." The result is the same. Just as the First Child of Mary, by His Passion, redeemed the very men and women who persecuted Him. So we other children of Mary, by our "passions," can yet save all who persecute us if we live ever "in Christ Jesus."

Many may say that is all very true about men like Cardinal Mindszenty, Bishop Ford, and those countless other martyrs of Europe and Asia, but how can we pose as helpers of God when we live in the relatively peaceful and religious America? After all we have seen on this Way, that question should never again be posed. For we have learned that the very Compassion of this Mother who is holding the dead hand of God would have been useless for salvation had it not been joined to the Passion of Jesus Christ. The death of any martyr is valueless apostolically unless that martyr is one with and in Jesus Christ and offers his all through the Christ.

We here in America, who have been baptized, are one

with Jesus Christ. We have seen the philosophical axiom about "actions belonging to the person!" Apply it to the mystical body of Christ and you will see the value of your most insignificant act! When we live "in Christ Jesus" all our acts are *sphered,* so to speak, in infinity. God takes them, and somehow makes them His own. Just as His hand lifted the daughter of Jairus from death; so we, if we become the right hand of God, can lift sinners from their death, open eyes born blind, unstop ears that have never heard melody, set the lame and halt walking and even running to God! And, in all truth, we become that right hand by becoming saints.

Let us go back again to the Mass and learn from this only important thing in all the world, the truly important lessons for all our lives.

This morning, I, and every priest who offered the Holy Sacrifice, took an almost weightless wafer of wheat, a drop of water, and a very insignificant amount of wine— three very ordinary, and truly insignificant things, no matter how we view them—and we offered them to God. Certainly in a world such as ours, these three things, plus the few words my fellow priests and I spoke, amount to nothing. Yet, when touched by God, when taken by Christ, when transubstantiated, what in the wide world can compare with them? Of the three things offered, neither you nor I, by ordinary vision, could see anything of the water; and of the wheat and the wine, the appearances remained just as insignificant after Consecration as before. But how deceiving are those appearances! The dynamism and power said to be latent in certain atoms, is as nothing compared to the Power in what looks like a tiny wafer of wheat and a half ounce of wine. Omnipotence is there. And so with our insignificant lives and the truly insignificant acts that fill them. Once they are placed in Christ Jesus, touched by God, taken into His Christ, they can save the world.

You may often have wondered why it is that God, who is justice Itself, does not blast our earth out of existence. If you ever sit in silence, look out over a city, and think of all the sin that goes on in it during a single night, you must tremble! For you have seen the first star of God's creation, Lucifer, the very light-bearer of the angelic hosts, hurled from heaven's threshold into the throat of hell for a single sin of pride. You have seen Eden closed to Adam and Eve, exile among beasts that are savage enemies decreed for our First Parents, and a long life of labor and misery and tears given as penance for their one sin of disobedience. You have seen but two of the hundreds of thousands God led out of Egypt allowed to enter the Promised land because of their idolatry and murmuring in the desert. You know of the Deluge, and have read of brimstone and fire that fell on Sodom and Gomorra. And you know something of the sin of the present day. Yes, you must tremble—and you must wonder.

God has not changed. He is still justice Itself. But our world has changed; changed entirely since a Mother sat with a limp white hand to her cheek late one Friday afternoon. That was the afternoon satisfaction enough for the sins of ten million worlds was offered to God. And it is that satisfaction that is offered day after day and all through the day all over the earth through water, wine, and a weightless wafer of wheat.

That truth brings out the necessity of putting your all in the Mass. Christ wants your insignificant acts! He will take them and offer them to God the Father as His own acts—and, as you know, there was nothing insignificant about the least act of Christ. It was powerful enough to redeem all mankind.

In the world today there is enough persecution of Christ going on to make all of us who love Him weep as Mary wept that first Good Friday. Yet the lesson we have been learning from these parallel lines that met is that our religion is a religion of joy; hence, every Christian, if he be a real Christian, must be an optimist. For the mystical body of Christ is a fact—and the Mass goes on!

Just as you can look out over a single city at night and imagine the hideous amount of sin that goes on in it, so you can look out over the world and realize the dazzling amount of holiness there is in it! A single Mass outweighs the evil of all time. One saint can outweigh a thousand, a hundred thousand, aye, even a million sinners. One soul that lives "in Christ Jesus" blinds the eye of God, as it were, to filth greater than Sodom's or ten thousand Gomorrhas. Sanctity is but another name for God; it spells Christ with different letters; it is the one real, positive power in the world. Sin and evil are negative; they have no true force. Especially since Christ died and His Mother held Him a corpse in her arms.

Sanctity is the atmosphere in which every Christian should "live and move and have his being." We were born into sanctity at baptism; we have been nourished by it in Holy Communion; we have been made strong in it by Confirmation; cured and rendered healthy again by Penance; kept in that atmosphere with all the gained strength and regained power thanks to the Holy Sacrifice of the Mass; and vast numbers of us have been placed in a state of sanctity by Matrimony or Holy Orders.

But we must not forget!

We are the salt of the earth—only if we are saints. We are the light of the world—only if we are saints. We are saviors of mankind—only if we live "in Christ Jesus." For He alone is holy—as we sing in the *Gloria* of the Mass. But, since baptism, there is no other way of life for us save "in Christ Jesus."

"Behold thy mother—" are words that speak of conquest even more than of a bequest. God took us to Himself that day by those words even as He gave us His Mother. So we must be holy with the very holiness of

God's only Son if we are to be true to our Mother and to
Christ.

I know it is frightening. I know also we must get over
our fright. For just as a man will never become a sailor if
he is afraid of the sea, nor an aviator if he fears to scorn the
earth and sail into thin blue air, so a Christian will never
become Christ if he shrinks from the heights and the
depths that make sanctity.

The Mother who holds the limp hand of God can free
us from our fright. She will; for she earned the right by
these dolors.

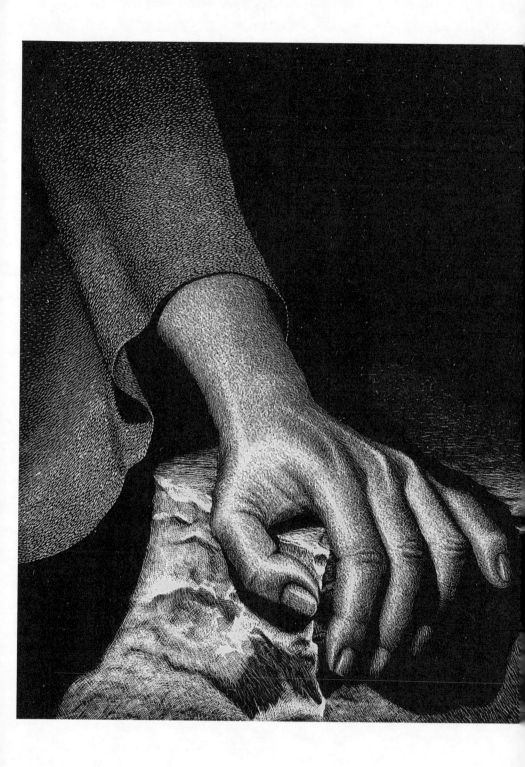

VII DOLOR

The Burial of Jesus

VIRGIN MOST FAITHFUL

"Joseph...laid him in a tomb which had been hewn
out of a rock. Then he rolled a stone to the entrance
of the tomb" (Mk. 15:46).

WE HAVE come the full length of the Way. We are at the
seventh dolor: the burial of that sacred body God had
taken from the immaculate womb of a Jewess and which
the Jews had silhouetted against a darkening sky—naked
and nailed. Now we see a Mother in the dusk with her
hand on the rock that hides that sacred body from her
sight. And all the world is dark.

Again and again, as we came along this Way, we have
been struck silent by the depths of the mystery that stood
before us and for the suffering of the Woman of all
women, whom we now call "Mother." We were struck
silent when Simeon pointed a bony hand to her heart and
told how it would be turned to a scabbard; when Joseph,
her husband, shook her out of sleep and hurried her into
Egypt; and again when the twelve-year-old Son of God let
her go off thinking He would be with His foster father,
and thus turned three days and three nights into agonies
no man can plumb. During the last three dolors, as we saw
the parallel lines meet, and Son and Mother undergo a
Passion and a Compassion that divide all Time, we could
not speak. What then shall we do as we view the climax of

all these dolors and see the Mother separated even from the dead body of her Son? The greatest sympathy and grandest love is often shown by silence. As we see her draw a reluctant hand away and watch her walk off into the deepening dusk, past those three stark, staring crosses, and head back into the City we can but love her without words, and worship her by our silence.

This is the deepest of all her deep dolors; for now she has nothing but her memories of Him who was her all. The approaching Sabbath will not allow her to linger and adore that which was dead. She must go back to the City and face what she had never faced since Gabriel had called her "full of grace." She must go back to Jerusalem and know that He was dead!

Not in Egypt, not when He was lost in the Temple, not during His public life, did she experience anything like what was in her heart and on her mind this Friday night, the fourteenth day of the month Nisan. Always before she could think of Him being some place, with some people. Now it would be near the Lake, now by the Jordan, then it would be in Samaria, or up the coast of Phoenicia by Tyre or Sidon. More often it was in Judea. But this dark night where was He? His sacred body, which she had prepared so hastily for the tomb, was hid behind rocks, and these had been sealed. She was all alone.

Those who have come back to an empty house after seeing a grave filled in know something of the emptiness there can be on our crowded earth. So long as the body of the loved one was in the house there was something of a presence, a nearness, and there was a deep, deep love. But once we have buried the corpse and come back to emptiness we know what death can do. Who can imagine the emptiness Mary found in that crowded City of Jerusalem that dark night which ushered in the Great Sabbath? Never since creation had the world seemed so void and empty. God had died that afternoon. God had been buried that evening. And Mary was God's Mother.

The last three dolors have had us on Calvary, present at the Mass. Since it is the Sacrifice which gives us the Sacrament, it was but natural that we should think much of the Eucharist as we watched the Virgin-Mother with the corpse in her arms. And since it is the Eucharist that gives us that Presence which fills our Churches with warmth and holiness, it will be His Absence from our Churches which will afford some insight into the empty world Mary knew as Friday's stars looked down on a city that had just killed God.

Our Basilica, here at Gethsemani, from the Mass of the Presanctified, which is now offered late Friday after-noon, until the Consecration of the Host in the Midnight Mass of the Easter Vigil, fills one with a sense of cold nakedness and the shame that accompanies such a state. I feel a chill, and the very clamminess which surrounds death, whenever I go in there and find altars stripped bare, sanctuary lamp dead, and the golden door of the taberna-cle swung wide to show us the yawning emptiness of the Holy of Holies. How utterly empty must Jerusalem have been the first Good Friday night, to Mary Immaculate and the sorrow that was in her heart.

"She was not ignorant," as St. Ambrose has said, "of the mystery that she had given birth to a child who was to rise from the dead." But let us not forget for an instant that the time of His Resurrection was still shrouded in mystery—even for Mary. Jesus had said again and again: "In three days." But who among the Jews could measure a day when that term falls from the lips of a Prophet of God, let alone when it comes from the mouth of God Himself? It could mean twenty-four hours as we measure time. It could also mean aeons, as it most likely means in the account of Creation. The fact remains that Mary was alone—and she knew not how long the loneliness would last. Her world was empty, and she knew not when He would fill it with His Presence again. The sanctuary lamp of her world was out and the tabernacle door stood ajar, showing no Host was there.

Mary was filled with sorrow as any mother would be who had seen her son condemned as a criminal and executed as Mary had seen her Son. Yet she was also filled with faith!

St. Thomas Aquinas has written that Saturday is dedicated to Mary because on the first Holy Saturday our world ever saw, she alone had perfect faith in the Redeemer, and in her alone the entire Faith of the Church remained from the time He died until He rose again.

Perhaps that is the lesson we moderns need to draw from this mysterious dolor: Faith! How often we allow our lights to dim when shadows fall! If our world is dark—and who can doubt that it is very dark?—is not the basic cause because so many have allowed the light of faith to fall?

THERE IS LIGHT— HOPE— HELP   A cloistered monk has very few contacts with those in the world. A letter now and then, a rare visit to a doctor, or a short hospitalization, about sums up his immediate contacts. But perhaps because he has been so isolated from the world, he sees it in better perspective when allowed a glimpse, and can take its pulse with greater accuracy than anyone continually in that world. I know I have been struck by the astounding lack of hope which youth shows concerning the future. I am convinced it is not a pose; it is genuine hopelessness. And it is that, perhaps more than anything else, which has generated a recklessness which has them grasping at the present moment with a greediness that frightens anyone who reflects. And in the adults I have found a feeling of helplessness which stirs the soul of anyone who knows what God has put in man. Never, never should hopelessness or a sense of helplessness seize one who has walked the dolorous way with Christ or the way of her dolors with Christ's Mother! Never should either be found in the soul of one who has been baptized in the Name of the Father, and of the Son, and of the Holy Ghost. For as St. Paul has said: "Faith is the foundation of the blessings for which we hope, the proof of the realities which we do not see" (Hebr. 11:1).[27]

Without Faith there can be no real hope, but with Faith there can never be hopelessness. Faith and faith alone, will give our youth genuine courage. That and that alone, will give birth to the fortitude they need to face life. And all our Faith rests ultimately on this rock which Mary was loathe to leave that first Good Friday night.

Let both our youth and our adults read and understand that eleventh chapter of St. Paul's Epistle to the Hebrews. It contains the secret of how to live bravely. The Apostle had coursed through Israelitic history from Abel to Rahab. He knew he had but scratched the surface. He also knew that what lay under the surface needed to be exposed, so he wrote: "Time will fail me if I try to go through all the history of Gedeon, of Barac, of Samson, of Jephte, of David and Samuel and the prophets. Theirs was the faith which subdued kingdoms, which served the cause of right, which made promises come true. They shut the mouths of lions, they quenched raging fire, swords were drawn on them, and they escaped. How strong they became, who till then were weak, what courage they showed in battle, how they routed invading armies! There were women, too, who recovered their dead children, brought back to life. Others, looking forward to a better resurrection still, would not purchase their freedom on the rack. And others experienced mockery and scourging, chains, too, and imprisonment; they were stoned, they were cut to pieces, they were tortured, they were put to the sword; they wandered about, dressed in sheepskins and goatskins, amidst want and distress and ill usage; men whom the world was unworthy to contain....One and all gave proof of their faith. (Hebr.11:32-39)[28]

---

[27] Kleist-Lilly translation.

That passage both stirs and shames us; for these men and women never saw what you and I have seen. They never knew the Christ or Christ's Mother! That was the whole point of Paul's argument, as is seen from his next chapter wherein be says: "Let us rid ourselves of all that weighs us down, of the sinful habit that clings so closely, and run, with all endurance, the race for which we are entered. Let us fix our eyes on Jesus, the origin and the crown of all faith, who, to win his prize of blessedness, endured the cross and made light of its shame, Jesus, who now sits on the right of God's throne (Heb. 12:1-2).[29]

This whole chapter is for us of the present day who have to face Communism and take it as a chastisement; and Ronald Knox translates the next verse in a way that fits in perfectly with the lesson we are trying to learn from this Dolor: "Take your standard from him [i.e., from Jesus], from his endurance, from the enmity the wicked bore him, and you will not grow faint, you will not find your souls unmanned."

I can well understand how in these days of black horizons any pagan, any unbeliever, whether young or old, would know real hopelessness and recognize his utter helplessness. But I can feel nothing but impatience with the hopeless attitude of those who believe in God and who know that He became man that men would never again be unmanned.

Listen further to St. Paul in Msgr. Knox's translation: "Your protest, your battle against sin, has not yet called for bloodshed; yet you have lost sight, already, of those words of comfort in which God addresses you as his sons; My son, do not undervalue the correction which the Lord sends thee, do not be unmanned when he reproves thy faults. It is where he loves that he bestows correction; there is no recognition of any child of his, without chastisement. Be patient, then, while correction lasts; God is treating you as his children. Was there ever a son whom his father

---

[28] Knox translation.

[29] Knox translation.

did not correct? No, correction is the common lot of all; you must be bastards, not true sons, if you are left without it. We have known what it was to accept correction from earthly fathers, and with reverence; shall we not submit, far more willingly, to the Father of a world of spirits, and draw life from him? They, after all, only corrected us for a short while, at their own caprice; he does it for our good, to *give us a share in that holiness which is his?*" (Heb. 4-10).

Do you see how that ties in with all we have said about sanctity as the goal of our lives? Do you begin to see why we can claim that Communism is a blessing? It will bring us bliss if we use it aright. It will make us saints if we face it as God wants it faced! It is His kindness to us who needed to be aroused.

What does God the Holy Ghost say to you this moment? Read on in St. Paul: "For the time being, all correction is painful rather than pleasant; but afterwards, when it has done its work of discipline, it yields a harvest of good dispositions, to our great peace. Come then, stiffen the sinews of drooping hand, and flagging knee, and plant your footprints in a straight track, so that the man who goes lame may not stumble out of the path, but regain strength instead. Your aim must be peace with all men, and that *holiness without which no one will ever see God*" (Heb. 12:11-14).[30]

All that manliness, all that strength of soul, all that vigor and real virtue are based on faith...faith in the God whom Paul says is "a consuming fire." Faith in such a God frees from all fears, gives courage and confidence in every crisis, stabilizes the soul when the whole world rocks, fills the mind and heart with peace and calm when all outside is chaos. For as Paul so pointedly asks: "Has not God said, 'I will never abandon or forsake you'?" and then concludes: "In complete trust then we can say:

---

[30] Knox translation. Emphasis added.

'The Lord is my helper;
I have nothing to fear.
What can man do to me?'" (Heb. 13:1-6)[31]

There is your explanation of what sustained Mary all this anguish-filled Friday and this cold and empty Saturday. It was faith! But never forget that Faith is not vision—a lesson our Lady taught with her whole life.

WHAT MARY SAW When she brought forth in the cave at Bethlehem she saw helplessness in human flesh; yet she adored in that helplessness the omnipotent God. What was it she carried into Egypt? A mere Infant, most likely still suckling at her breast; yet she adored in Him the Maker of the world. What did she see at Nazareth save only a Boy who had to learn from Joseph how to handle a hammer, a saw, and a plane; yet she adored Omniscience in that little One being thus taught. Mary's life was a life of faith, of fortitude and fidelity. It took great strength of mind and will never to waver in her belief that the Infant, the Boy, and the Man who called her "Mother" was also her God. It allowed for no forgetfulness of the fact that God had spoken to her through Gabriel. But what a test of faith, fortitude, and fidelity were those three hours on Calvary!

She saw a human Being hammered to a cross. To human eyes how did Jesus differ from the thieves who were condemned and crucified with Him? If some stranger had come to Jerusalem that Friday afternoon and passed Calvary before darkness enfolded it, how could he tell that the middle cross held Innocence and the Redemption of mankind? He would have seen three naked men dying by degrees. How could he know that One was not only the Light of the World but the Life of all living? Mary had eyes of flesh and she saw the beaten, bloody body of her Son upon the nails. She saw that body taken down. She held it. She counted the wounds. She untangled the blood-matted hair. She folded the nerveless arms. She closed the gaping

---

[31] Kleist-Lilly translation.

mouth. She straightened the lifeless legs. She knew she was holding a corpse. Yet in that corpse she adored the Christ of God and the Jesus of men. Was there ever such faith on earth? Was it not this which gave her such fortitude and made her the "Virgin Most Faithful"? Was it not her fortitude that strengthened and ever strengthened her unfaltering faith?

Have you ever pondered on how she reacted to these events that make Holy Week such a soul-searching and so soul-shaking an experience? Do you know of any other mother who would not have cried condemnation on the perfidy of Judas, the thief who would sell his Master for thirty pieces of silver? Can you conceive any other mother who would not say it had been the hate of the high priests, the jealousy of the Scribes and Pharisees, the resentment of the powerful that had brought her Son to the cross? Would it not be natural for a mother to cry shame on the weakness of a man like Pontius Pilate who again and again returned a verdict of "Not Guilty," yet finally gave Him over to the executioners? And what if she had charged the soldiers with heartlessness and Longinus with cold cruelty would it not have been what you would expect from a mother?

We find none of these in Scripture or tradition. No legend lives to say that Mary was anything but silent. And in that silence she was adoring the will of God and accepting His all-wise and all-loving plan. Judas with his kiss and his thirty pieces of silver, Annas with his cunning, Caiphas with his cruelty, the Sanhedrin with its shameful servility, even Pilate with his lack of principle and Herod with his lusts—all fitted into God's permissive Providence. And while each drove a sword into her heart, each gave wider scope to her faith and greater worth to her adoration.

If we are going to walk the Way our Mother walked, we will need a faith that will give us fortitude; and a fortitude that will make us the very souls of fidelity.

The test of our trueness to our Mother and our God is made when trials, or what we call "crosses," come our way. When we are found with tuberculosis, cancer, or some similar disease, do we bless God, adore His will, accept it lovingly as part of His all-wise plan? When our best efforts meet with failure, when frustration and unqualified defeat are common experiences, when friends prove untrue and loved ones are taken by death, do we glorify God, see His hand in all such happenings, clasp it, kiss it, and from a sincere heart say: *Fiat Voluntas Tua?* When those in power give us as much chance as Jesus had before Annas and Caiphas, when they laugh us to scorn as Herod did Him, when they condemn us as unjustly as Pilate did the Christ, do we take the word God used to create the world, the word Mary used to bring into flesh Him who would re-create it, the word Jesus used at the beginning of His Great Act of Redemption? Do we say *Fiat?* It is the one word that expresses fullest faith. It is the one word that demands highest fortitude. It is the only word that spells real fidelity. Mary used it and became Mother of God. We must use it if we will be true to our God and our Mother. That is the lesson of this hand on the rock.

Of course there will be those who will object and say we cannot have faith like Mary's because she was in possession of a fact that made her faith easy. She knew she was the Mother of God. She knew that she had conceived by the Holy Ghost. That fact changed her outlook on life and all things in life.

That is true. There was never a moment of her years on earth whether at Bethlehem, in Egypt, at Nazareth, or on Calvary that she was not conscious of her virginity and consequently of her divine maternity. That fact did change her whole outlook.

But have we not as great a fact? Have we not this sealed tomb on which her hand rests? Do we not know it was empty Sunday morning? There is the rock on which our

Faith is founded. There is the rock which gives stability greater than that of Gibraltar. The fact that this rock was found empty, despite guards and seals, should be as pivotal to all our thinking as was Mary's consciousness of the way she had conceived. We *know* that the Christ who was crucified rose from the dead. He promised it. He gave it as the proof of His divinity. Peter, Paul, and all the Apostles preached it as the bedrock of Christianity. History and severest historical criticism have proclaimed it as fact. Why then should we hesitate a fraction of a second to say *Fiat* to anything and everything that transpires?

If God be God nothing can happen without His willing it. He can will it absolutely, conditionally, or merely permissively. His Providence over this world of ours is called directive, permissive, or preventive according to the way He wills different affairs. But it is the fact that we need to focus on, not the form of His willing. So long as God, who is all good, wills a thing, we are fools if we do not say *Fiat*—and thus will it with Him. The lone exception is sin—God never wills that. But that He can draw good from the evil he permits is evident from the corpse with the five ugly wounds which He transformed into a glorified body glowing with five radiant memorials of His Passion.

A THEOLOGY FOR LIFE

Because Mary knew that Jesus was God she could say a silent *Fiat* to the kiss of Judas, the condemnation of Pilate, the lance thrust of Longinus. Because we know Jesus is God we can say *Fiat* in the face of the cruelest tyranny.

Because Mary knew she had conceived God, not only the sound of iron beating on iron but the utter silence of the tomb all day Saturday spoke to her of God's glory. Because we know that tomb was empty on Sunday, we will say *Fiat* and give glory to God even when God has to go underground. For we are certain that the "gates of Hell shall not prevail!" We are positive that "in the end her heart will triumph!" We are convinced and even persuaded that "every child of God has enough strength to become a victor over the world; and this is the victory that has conquered the world, our faith" (Jn. 5:4).[32]

At this moment of history and section of God's eternal plan there is a whole world to be combated and conquered by our Faith and for our Faith. It is the world that knows not Christ—or knowing Him, condemns Him again to the cross, crying as they cried of old: "Away with Him! Away with Him! We have no king but Caesar."

We sons of God and children of Mary belong to the Church *Militant*. Hence, we can never be noncombatants! The *Fiat* I have been urging you to make your life's motto, far from connoting mere passivity, is more frequently a fierce declaration of war. It is acceptance of the "status quo" that God has seen fit to permit; but it is at the same time a rejection of every atom of evil in that status, which God most certainly does not want. It is essential that we firmly grasp the truth that what God merely permits, He really does not want! Failing to grasp that, we will fail to understand this doctrine of *Fiat,* and we shall fail to live the life God wants us to live and Mary showed us how to achieve. God permits sin; He certainly does not want it. He permits us to know temptation; He expects us to reject it. He permits heresy and schism; He ardently desires that we combat and conquer the one and heal the other. At this moment of time He permits Communism; He most certainly wills that we war against it with every power of mind and heart, every energy of body and soul, every faculty and fiber of our being. What God merely permits, He most certainly does not want.

Understand, then, the world of meaning in that tiny word *Fiat.* When Mary used it she meant she was going to *co-operate* with God in His mighty works of the Incarnation and the Redemption. When we use it, and we should use it all the time, it means much the same; it

---

[32] Kleist-Lilly translation.

means that we are going to co-operate with God in the prolongation of His Incarnation and in the continuation of His Redemption. It means that we are living and laboring for the one only purpose of completing His mighty work of salvation.

Understood in that sense—and that is the only sense in which it should be understood—that tiny word, meaning: "Thy Will be done, O God," calls for action.

The sublime doctrine of abandonment, or conformity to the will of God, will inevitably make saints—but only if it is rightly understood. Conformity to the will of God is not mere passive acceptance of everything that is; it most frequently is opposition to things that are, because they are by God's so-called "permissive will." The most exact of theologians always make sharp distinction—such as Schouppe does in his *Dogmatic Theology*—and stress the fact that "The Will that we name permissive, according to which God allows sin and its consequences to be, is *wrongly* called a Will. Because God does *not will* those evils. He merely tolerates them." What these theologians simply declare, the Council of Trent solemnly defined. In its sixth session it said: "If any man claims that God works evil as He works good, and not merely permissively,...let him be anathema." Then the Council did what councils seldom do, it gave an example. It declared: "If any man says that the betrayal by Judas was the will and work of God as was the conversion of Saul...let him be anathema." The council is saying that what God merely permits, He does not will. And she is telling us that our *Fiat* will call for action much more than for mere acceptance in such circumstances as those in which we find the world today.

Do not think I am departing from my theme that you are to make the Mass your life and your life a Mass. Do not forget God opened His Mass with the *Fiat* of Gethsemani. And realize that your *Fiat* will mean that you are entering into Communion with God Almighty. It will mean that you want to make His will your will; that you two will be one in willing and not willing the same thing at the same time.

Mary, by taking us on her Way has given us much more than a way of life, much more than a mere philosophy of life; she has given us what each of us needs: a *theology* for life.

GOD KNOWS WHAT HE IS ABOUT Since we have been made His members, it is a theology of life we need and not a mere philosophy. God is our life! But we so often forget! Now, however, after walking this Way, let us never again forget that *God knows what He is about!*

That is the fact that gave Mary her fortitude and her fidelity. It is the fact based on faith. And it is that fact which will spark our wills to speak that word which is adoration, acceptation, expiation, reparation, and petition all in one—*Fiat.* Our word is entirely "Eucharistic"—for when we use it, it consecrates our deeds as the words of the priest consecrate wheat and wine. More, it communicates —for it gives God to us and gives us to God!

We are never again to forget, that every event in our lives is a *coming of Christ.* Let it never be said again that "He came unto His own and His own received Him not." We are to receive Him in everything and everyone! We will do so only if we remember that He is God who was born outside Juda's least of cities and done to death outside her greatest; that He is God who at birth had to borrow a manger to be laid in, and at death was laid in a borrowed tomb; that He is God who became a poor man, a Man of Sorrows well acquainted with all our infirmities; that He is the God-Man who led such a lowly, lonely life, who knew hunger and thirst as we know them, who was stung by ingratitude greater than we will ever have to bear, who faced opposition fiercer far than anything we will ever know, who met frustration, failure, and defeat, and went back to God with, it would seem, only a thief as the garner of all His years and all His labors! That is the Christ who comes to us in every event of our lives. Since He is Jesus Christ, the same yesterday, today, and forever, we can expect Him to come to us in the garb of lowliness, loneliness, opposition, ingratitude, frustration, failure, and defeat; for it was by such things that He redeemed the world—and it will be by such things that we will help Him save it!

History repeats itself. But our work is to reverse the history of the Chosen People of God. God will repeat His work—for He is immutable. But we are to learn from what the Jews failed to learn. Our darkness is to comprehend the Light. When He comes to His own, we are to receive Him. God is leading us as He led the Jews; for there is a clear-cut unity to God's plan, and His whole purpose is expressed in that high-priestly prayer of Christ: "That they may be one in Us."...But mankind is slow to learn and seems ever unready to accept the gift of God—that unity with Him who is Life.

To win us God has first to wean us, and wean us from all that is not God. The most cursory reading of the Old Testament makes this plan of God evident. He was ever trying to give His People a *sense of God*—the thing our sorry modern world so tragically needs.

Primitive man and primitive Israel had a sense of God, but it was a totally false one. To them everything was God, and nothing was God. They divinized almost everything, yet never came anywhere near the true Divine One. Every promontory, every tree on a hilltop, every grove, every spring was, for them, a hidden and awe-compelling presence of something or someone divine. You can see that their instinct was right; for God is immanent, He is omnipresent. Yet, fundamentally they were grossly wrong; for God is transcendent; and these poor primitives were adoring the creature as if it were the Creator. It was idolatry. It was a transgression of the First Commandment God was later to give Moses, and a violation of that Command which God has written in our minds and hearts. We have an instinct for God. Adoration is something innate to us. But we are children of parents who sinned. So our intellects are not as bright as they would have been, nor our wills as strong. We often go astray by what is innate and instinctive.

Reading the Old Testament we are conscious of a sustained tension; finally we awake to the fact that God is really wrestling with His people, and without destroying their freedom, He is all but compelling them to recognize Him as the one true God. But the Jews were ever slipping from His grasp. Whenever they came in contact with the Egyptians, Canaanites, or Babylonians, back they went to idols. But God who is Love and the God who will not be mocked went on wrestling. He sent prophet after prophet—and finally sent His Son. This determination of God to win wayward man explains the history of Israel as nothing else can explain it. They knew captivity, concentration camps, mass murder, and every horror that makes our day so horrible not only as a just chastisement, but also and ultimately as a loving Father's enticement to bring His prodigal sons and daughters home again.

The Jews never understood God's way with them. They heard His promises and took them to mean happiness on earth, mastery over other nations, material prosperity. But God was only trying to give them Himself!

To shock them into sensibility, He sent them suffering. It was His weaning process. He would wean them from those things to which they were so ardently attached; He would wean them from the things they were most fond of; He would empty them so that He might fill them with Himself. That is why the Kingdom was split and Israel was taken by the Assyrians, and Juda went off to Babylon a captive.

A remnant came back and Jerusalem was again

crowned by a Temple. But this Way of Mary's which met her Son's shows how unsuccessful God was in His effort to fill His Chosen People with His very own life. They would not have the Messias whose Kingdom was not of this world. They would not say *Fiat!*

God is trying to wean and win us today with the same tactics He used on the Jews. We have had scourges of all kinds from world-wide wars to world-wide economic depressions; we have had epidemics that crossed oceans and carried millions to the grave. We now experience a concentration of all these scourges in a thing we call Communism, and all I can hear from that malevolent thing is the voice of Isaias, Jeremias, Ezechiel, and Daniel, the voice of all the other prophets, the very voice of God Himself saying: "They shall know that I am the Lord their God—They shall not have strange gods before Me!"

The mystery of the present time is no new mystery. It is simply the primordial mystery of Creation. God said: "Let us make man to our image and likeness" (Gen. 1:26). He did. But man soon marred that likeness and obscured that image. But God would not give in. Christ came. He said: "I came that they may have life, and have it more abundantly" (Jn. 10: 10). We have seen Him win that life for us by His death. And now we know that Christ is ever coming into souls of men, of nations, and of the world. But men, and nations, and the world will conceive Christ only if they say what Mary said to Gabriel. We of the twentieth century will "mother" Christ only if we say *Fiat*—and say it most especially to suffering and sorrow. The excruciating pains of our day need not be those of a death-agony; they are meant by God to be the pangs of birth—the birth of Christ in all of us. That is why Mary is so important to the mystery of our times.

She played a leading part in the birth of the Physical Body of the God-Man; she played a leading part in its growth; she played a leading part in its death which was its

I SAW THE MORNING BREAK

triumph. She will play the same part, the leading part, in the birth, the growth, and the death and the triumph of the Mystical Body of the same Christ. That is why I have insisted from the beginning that the two truths—We are His members, and she is our Mother—are really one.

Her hand on this tomb teaches us many lessons, but the essential one for us to learn right now is that just as Mary became our Mother by a suffering in her heart as wide and deep as the suffering Jesus knew in His body, so we will prove His members only if we allow Him to enlarge the narrow limits of our human hearts until they swell unto the wide compass of His Sacred Heart; and He can do that, it would seem, only if like Mary we say *Fiat* to all suffering. Nothing in the nature of trouble, trial, sorrow should ever present us with a problem again; for we have seen that it was through suffering that Jesus redeemed the world; through like suffering that Mary became its Co-Redemptrix; and that if we are to be Christians, we will use the identical means to save mankind.

By way of parenthesis let me say that this hand on the tomb has a lovely lesson for all those unfortunate members of Christ who have fallen into mortal sin. In them Jesus lies dead—as dead as He was on this Sabbath of twenty centuries ago. But on them, as on this tomb, the hand of Mary, the Refuge of Sinners, rests, awaiting and praying for the Resurrection of Christ within them! May those who are in such a state feel that hand as they read this book, and bring Christ to life within them by asking Mary to help them make a perfect act of contrition, which is an act of love, this moment. She can grant such a grace; for she is Mediatrix of all grace!

Raoul Plus, S.J., ended a small book on Mary with the words: "We are inclined to believe the world is only at its beginning (not at its end). For the Gospel is just beginning to shine. Everything is yet to be done. It is not an end, therefore, that is foreshadowed, but an aurora that is rising. The world wants more Evangelical substance, and in those places where the Gospel has already penetrated, more Evangelical life. In this conquest who will aid most efficaciously, both in extent and in depth?—Mary!"[33]

Who will dare say, after LaSalette, Lourdes, Pontmain, and Fatima, that Mary does not stand outside the tomb which is the modern world, with her hand resting there awaiting the Resurrection of the Christ? This hand on the rock can give us all that is needed. It should awaken in us now a faith that will be dauntless even when the whole world is dark; for it will tell us that Golgotha's dusk was but prelude to Sunday's glorious dawn; that the scarred human corpse of Christ was a necessary condition for the impassible glorified body, into the wounds of which Thomas put his finger and probed with his fist; that the crown of thorns was purchase price for the halo of light and loveliness the women saw around His head when they met Him outside the tomb.

Mary's hand on this rock says to us:

Ye that have faith to look with fearless eyes
    Beyond the tragedy of a world at strife,
And trust that out of night and death shall rise
    The dawn of ampler life;
Rejoice, whatever anguish rend your heart,
    That God has given you for a priceless dower,
To live in these great times and have your part
    In Freedom's crowning hour;
That you may tell your sons who see the light
    High in the heavens—their heritage to take—
"I saw the powers of Darkness put to flight,
    I saw the Morning break."[34]

Only those will see the morning break who look on Mary; for Mary is the Morning Star! Only those will see the Powers of Darkness put to flight who lean on Mary;

[33] *Mary in Our Soul-Life* (Pustet, 1940), p.152.

[34] "Between Midnight and Morning," by Owen Seaman. From *Masterpieces of Religious Verse* (New York: Harper and Brothers, 1948).

for she is the Woman whom God spoke of in Genesis after He had cursed the snake saying: "I will put enmities between thee and the woman, and thy seed and her seed: she shall crush thy head, and thou shall lie in wait for her heel" (Gen. 3:15). Only those will pass on this happy heritage to their sons who imitate Mary; for she is the Woman of the Apocalypse, the one whom John saw as the great sign that appeared in the heavens: "a woman that wore the sun for her mantle, with the moon under her feet, and a crown of twelve stars about her head. She had a child in her womb, and was crying out as she travailed, in great pain of her delivery. Then a second portent appeared in heaven; a great dragon was there, fieryred...and he stood fronting the woman...ready to swallow up the child as soon as she bore it. She bore a son, the son who is to herd the nations like sheep with a crook of iron..." (Apoc. 12:1-5).

Let St. Pius X have the final word as he interprets these two signs.

"No one is ignorant," he writes in Ad *Diem Illum,* "that this woman signified the Virgin Mary, who remained inviolate when she brought forth our Head....So John saw the most holy Mother of God already enjoying happiness, yet travailing in a kind of mysterious childbirth. What birth was this? Clearly it was the birth of us who are still detained in exile and yet to be generated to the perfect charity of God and to eternal happiness. And the labors in the childbirth show the desire and love with which the Virgin on her throne watches over us and strives with unceasing prayer to complete the number of the elect."

We are His members! She is our Mother! Mary's dolors not only give us courage; they give us joy! Her hand is on the rock; He shall arise!

Mater Divinae Gratiae

MATER MISERICORDIAE

WHAT worlds of thought the briefest contemplation of Mary opens up!

We have spent Holy Week walking her Way—and found ourselves back with the Trinity before Creation and ahead with the Trinity after the Last Judgment. It is inevitable. For Mary is the glory of that Trinity: daughter of the Father, Mother of the Son, and Spouse of the Holy Spirit—and she is our Mother, we poor humans who must be judged, we poor mortals who are to put on immortality. And though it is true to say that in one sense Mary is outside of Time, we have seen from these dolors how pertinent she is to our times. She frees us from fear; she fills us with faith; she fires us with such hope that we look upon our day as one of happiest opportunity to do something great for God.

We opened by saying: "Our hope lies in the hands of a woman." We close by saying: " It lies in the hands of that woman who held Christ at Bethlehem; the hands that carried Him into Egypt; the hands that helped Him grow at Nazareth; the hands that received Him from the cross and swathed His body for the burial."

We have tried to learn many timely lessons from these hands as we walked with her on her Way, but we would have missed the most important lesson for our times if we failed to learn that it is from these hands that we are to receive all grace. We would have walked with her in vain if we did not see that by these dolors she became our *Alma Mater* in the strictest sense of that term; for she merited, under Christ, through, in, and with Christ all the graces mankind is to know. By her compassion she won for herself the role of *Mediatrix of all Grace* and the titles that mean so much to us men: Mother of Grace and Mother of Mercy.

Back in the twelfth century St. Bernard of Clairvaux said: "God has willed that we receive all things through Mary." This great Doctor of the Church was voicing soundest theology and showing us the way to God: it is through Mary. Now granting that the way to God the Father is through the Son, since Jesus told us so—"No one comes to the Father except through me,"—we must realize that the way to the Son is through His Mother. And I believe Jesus told us that, too; it was in her fifth dolor when He said: "Woman, behold thy son. Son, behold thy Mother."

THE POPES GIVE TESTIMONY   Leo XIII, in his encyclical *Octobri Mense,* wrote: "How great are the goodness and mercy revealed in this design of God! What a boon to the frailty of man! We believe in the infinite goodness of the Most High, and we rejoice in it; we believe also in His justice, and we fear it. We adore the beloved Saviour who generously gave His blood; but at the same time we dread the inexorable judge. Thus do those whose actions have disturbed their consciences need an intercessor mighty in favor with God, merciful enough not to reject the cause of the desperate, merciful enough to lift up again toward hope in the divine mercy the afflicted and the broken. Mary is this glorious intermediary. *She is the mighty Mother of God.* But—what is still sweeter—she is gentle, exquisite in tenderness, and of a limitless love and kindness. *As such God gave her to us.*"[35]

That this Mother of Divine Grace is Mother of Mercy

---

[35] Emphasis added.

Leo teaches in the very next lines: "Having chosen her for the mother of His only-begotten Son, He taught her all a mother's feeling that breathes nothing but pardon and love. Such Christ desired she should be, for He consented to be subject to Mary and to obey her as a son a mother. And such He proclaimed her from the cross when He entrusted to her care and love the whole race of man in the person of His disciple John. As such, finally, does she prove herself by her courage in gathering the heritage of the enormous labors of her Son, and in accepting the charge of her Son, and in accepting the charge of her maternal duties toward us all."

In another encyclical, "The Mighty Mother of God" *Magnae Dei Matris*—this same Pope wrote: "When we have recourse to Mary in prayer, we are having recourse to the Mother of Mercy, who is so well disposed toward us that, whatever the necessity that presses upon us, especially in attaining eternal life, she is instantly at our side, even though she has not been invoked. She dispenses grace with a generous hand from that treasure with which from the beginning she was divinely endowed in fullest abundance that she might be worthy to be the Mother of God. By the fullness of grace which confers on her the most illustrious of her many titles, the Blessed Virgin is infinitely superior to all the hierarchies of men and angels, the one creature who is closest of all to Christ. 'It is a great thing in any saint to have grace sufficient for the salvation of many souls; but to have enough for the salvation of everybody in the world is the greatest of all; and this is found in Christ and in the Blessed Virgin.'"

It is fascinating to study the furrow Mary has cut across our century not only with her many appearances to mother us with real mercies, but also by the way she has grown in the liturgy and life of the Church, the way the learned theologians and each of the Sovereign Pontiffs have spoken of her. Leo XIII never tired of writing on her.

He gave us eleven different encyclicals on her Rosary—and in each you can find passages which show her as Mother of Mercy and Mother of all Grace. St. Pius X, the beloved Pontiff (whose canonization highlighted the Marian Year just passed) gave us *Ad Diem Illum,* from which I have quoted often as I contemplated these ink drawings of her Way. In that document he said that "upon her, as upon a foundation, the noblest after Christ, rises the edifice of the Faith of all centuries." That is certainly high praise; but it is only the beginning of the panegyric that Pius preached. He went on to her function in the Mystical Body and used that figure of which the early Fathers were so fond—"For she is the neck of our Head by which He communicates to His Mystical Body all spiritual gifts. We are thus, it will be seen, very far from declaring the Mother of God to be the authoress of supernatural grace. Grace comes from God alone. But since she surpassed all in holiness and union with Christ, and has been associated by Christ in the work of Redemption, she, as the expression is, merits *de congruo* what Christ merits *de condigno,* and is the principal minister in the distribution of grace. He sitteth at the right hand of the Majesty on high; but Mary sitteth as a queen on His right hand, the securest refuge of those who are in peril, as well as the most faithful of helpers, so that we have nought to fear or despair of, as long as she is our guide and our patroness; she is our defender and protector."

The concluding line of that memorable encyclical runs: "True we are passing through disastrous times, when we may well make our own the lamentation of the Prophet: 'There is no truth, and there is no mercy, and there is no knowledge of God in the land. Cursing, and lying, and killing, and theft, and adultery have overflowed' (Osee 4:1-2). Yet in the midst of this deluge of evil, the Virgin Most Clement rises before our eyes like a rainbow, as the arbiter of peace between God and man. 'I will set my bow in the clouds, and it shall be the sign of a covenant between me and between the earth' (Gen. 9:13). Let the storm rage and the sky darken—not for that shall we be dismayed. 'And the bow shall be in the clouds, and I shall see it and shall remember the everlasting covenant' (Gen. 9:16). 'And there shall no more be waters of a flood to destroy all flesh' (Gen. 9:15). Oh yes, if we trust as we should in Mary, now especially...we shall recognize in her the Virgin most Powerful, 'who with virginal foot did crush the head of the serpent.'"[36]

His successor, Benedict XV, in his letter "On the Queen of Peace" addressed to his Secretary of State, in the midst of World War I wrote: "And since all the graces which God deigns to bestow in pity upon men are dispensed through Mary, We urge that in this terrible hour, the trusting petitions of her most afflicted children be directed to her. We direct Your Eminence to make known to all the Bishops of the world that it is our fervent desire that mankind turn to the Sacred Heart of Jesus—the Throne of Grace—and that recourse to this Throne be made through Mary. Accordingly, We ordain that, beginning with the first day of June this year, there be placed in the Litany of the Blessed Virgin the invocation: *Queen of Peace, pray for us...*"

There is the source of that beautiful title for Mary— also of the Feast of Mary, Mediatrix of All Grace.

Ten years after Benedict had given us the Feast of Mediatrix of All Grace, Pius XI was writing his *Lux Veritatis*. It is a sturdy work and characteristic of this fearless Pontiff. In one part he says: "...let us trust to her confidently all that is ours—joys, if we rejoice; woes, if we are in trial; hopes, if we endeavor to rise to nobler things. If the Church falls on difficult times; if faith wanes and charity grows cold; if morals, private and public, deteriorate; if any danger threatens the Catholic cause or civil society, let us have recourse to her, begging help from heaven; and in

---

[36] Office of the Immaculate Conception.

the supreme trial of death, when all hope, all help, is gone, let us lift up our eyes in tears and trembling, imploring through her pardon from her Son and eternal joy in heaven."

In late 1937, when the world was expecting news of his death, Pius XI wrote from Castel Gandolfo his plea for the Rosary and our devotedness to Mary. It is called *Ingravescentibus Malis* and in it he says that for "the increasingly grave evils of our times there is no remedy but in the return of mankind to Christ." Then he shows that the way back is through Mary. He quotes, as so many before him had quoted, my father, St. Bernard: "Such is the Will of God, that we should have all things through Mary."

Permit me to quote here the beautiful words that are found in Ecclesiasticus: "I am the mother of fair love, and of fear, and of knowledge, and of holy hope. In me is all grace of the way and of the truth, in me is all hope of life and of virtue. Come over to me all ye that desire me, and be filled with my fruits" (Ecclus. 24:24-26).

The fruits we of this mad mid-twentieth century most need are those of faith, fortitude, and fidelity. She can give them; for she is *Mater Divinae Gratiae et Mater Misericordiae;* she is the merciful Mother who holds in her tender, generous hand all grace! She is the Virgin Most Powerful! And she is our Mother!

WE ARE AT THE BEGINNING —NOT THE END Now that you have walked with this Woman from the day she carried her Child to the Temple (as an "*Introit*" to His Mass) unto the day when she carried His corpse to the tomb (after He had sung His "*Ite, Missa Est*"); now that you have seen how she was foretold in Genesis and foreshadowed by all the great women of the Old Testament from Eve to the Mother of the Machabees; now that you have seen how she became the Mother of all Men and have heard one Pontiff describe her as "sitting at the right hand of Him who sitteth at the right hand of God," and another define her Assumption into Heaven and make ready the proclamation of her universal Queenship, do you not realize that Mary of Nazareth, the young Maid who said *Fiat* and sang *Magnificat,* is the focal point of the universe; that "all generations have and yet will call her Blessed"; that in her the angels find gladness, the just grace, and the sinners, pardon; that to her all in heaven, all in purgatory, and all the wise of earth look; that, as St. Thomas has so well said: "she borders on the Infinite"—for by her very being she bears most intimate relation with the Father, whose Eternal Paternity she shared in Time; with the Son, whose *Kenosis*—emptying of self—and consequent triumph she made possible by becoming His Mother; with the Holy Ghost, who overshadowed her for the birth of the Physical Christ, came down upon her in the Cenacle for the Epiphany of the Mystical Christ, and who now overflows through her on all Christ's members in the world?

St. Grignon de Montfort declared that the last days of the world would be full of Mary's presence, and that a renewal of devotion to her would be the preparation for the conversions—for that *metanoia* so necessary for man—that would precede the final cataclysms. Because of her appearances: in Paris in 1830, when she gave us the Miraculous Medal on which she is shown with hands widespread from which stream copious flashes of light, symbolic of the graces she sheds on mankind; at LaSalette, where she wept and asked us to keep holy the Sabbath day—that mystical reminder not only of the resting of God after Creation but of that eternal rest we all hope to enjoy with God on that Sabbath which will know no end; at Lourdes, where she revealed the mystery of her Immaculate Conception, that gift of God which fitted her to Mother His Christ, and where she now works marvels and miracles as great as the Angel of the Pool at Bethsaida ever worked; at Fatima, where she came as the Lady of

Light, to call us to such a *metanoia* that we would not only glorify God by our prayer and penance, but we would save men from the upraised arm of an outraged God—because of these visible appearances, I say, and of those invisible ones in souls she sanctifies, manifested to some degree in the ever growing Legion of Mary, in her generous, self-sacrificing Blue Army, in her stalwart sodalists and her countless followers who wear her scapular and her miraculous medal, many think that St. Grignon's prophecy is being fulfilled. But there are others who say: "No, we are only at the beginning!" And if statistics mean anything, these latter seem more right; for Christ is yet to come in more than half the world!

We have seen that there is strict unity in God's plan. Why can it not be, then, that this newer, more keenly felt presence of Mary in our world is but prelude to a newer Pentecost? Mary was important not only for the coming of Christ but for the coming of the Holy Ghost. Was it not through her that He was poured out in the Incarnation, *"Spiritus Domini superveniet in te*—The Spirit of God shall come upon thee"; was it not through her, in some fashion, that He was poured out in the Cenacle, *"Et erat mater Jesu ibi*—and the Mother of Jesus was there"? Very much so! It was with her, as the Acts tell us, that the Apostles persevered in prayer. So will it not be through her that He will come again into the souls of men and into the heart of the world? Are we not now at the dawn of a new Age: that of Mary and of the Mystical Body of Christ?

She did tell us at Fatima that "in the end my Heart will triumph!" Can it not be that we are at the beginning of that end? Can it not be that the darkness now over all the world is but that deeper darkness we always know before dawn? Can it not be the harbinger of the coming of Our Lady of Light—the Lady of Sorrows with whom we have spent Holy Week, and with whom we wish to spend eternity as the Cause of our Joy?

On the last day at Fatima, October 13, 1917, Lucy was granted many different visions of our lovely Mother. The one that should speak to us who have contemplated her Way is the final one which was of Our Lady of Sorrows. But—and here is the point of this book and of these masterly drawings—Lucy looked closely at the heart of our Sorrowful Mother that day and found that *there was no sword in her heart!*

Raoul Plus, S.J., in his book *Mary in Our Soul-Life* tells the story which he calls "The Legend of the Eighth Sword." It is one that may well haunt us all the remaining days of our exile....There was once a young man who was accustomed to visit Our Lady of the Seven Dolors every day. But one sad day he fell into grievous sin. When he made his usual visit to the Madonna that day he was startled to see in her heart not seven, but *eight* swords! He needed no explanation. He rose from his knees and sought a priest. His confession was humble, sincere, integral, and filled with deepest sorrow. He arose with resolution burning in his quickened soul. He returned to his Madonna and smiled through his tears when he saw that the eighth sword had disappeared.

A legend, of course; but how it points out for us our work in life! We are His members! She is our Mother! We have a work to do! We have indeed "something to live for and something for which we are ready to die!" We have a Faith and a Vision! Our work is not only to take the eighth sword from our Mother's heart, but to take all the other seven! For we have seen that His body bleeds! Hence, our Mother weeps! She pointed the Way to save the world. It is by the Mass. We must make the Mass—which is Christ—our life, and our lives a Mass!

For the last time let me quote Pascal, but this time let me quote him fully: "Jesus will be in agony until the end of the world—*we must not sleep the while!*"